FORCES
OF CHANGE

FORCES OF CHANGE

Transformational Nonprofit Stories Of Leaders Who Are Paving
The Way For Others To Take Action

Compiled by Cathy Staton

Co-authors: Letitia Council, Nadine Owens, Nischelle Buffalow, Ronjeanna Harris, Tanikwa S. Matthews, and Veronica
McMillian

Warren, Michigan
United States of America

CONTENTS

ACKNOWLEDGMENTS

Cathy Staton: All the Glory goes to God. I bless Him for giving me such an amazing vision to execute.

I thank the amazing contributing authors Letitia Council, Ronjeanna Harris, Tanikwa Matthews, Nadine Owens, Nischelle Buffalow, and Veronica for sharing their hearts and stories of change. Thank you for believing and trusting me to assist you with sharing your stories.

We are eternally grateful to Tucker Publishing House, LLC, Tara Tucker, and her team for helping us refine our ideas and approach throughout the creative process. This book is richer for your contributions.

We thank our families for putting up with us for the time it has taken to bring this project to fruition. I want to thank my readers who have stuck with me through it all.

We want to give a big shout-out to all the amazing volunteers who give of themselves and time and donors who assist nonprofits with changing the world one person at a time.

Thank you to the nonprofits who strive to help people who need us the most. Thank you for putting books to the ground. Thank you for all that you do to help bring about change in the world. May your nonprofits not only survive but thrive.

Letitia Council: I would like to take the time to acknowledge God first for this amazing opportunity to become the author He knew that I would become. God, thank you for believing and seeing the best there was in me. Thank you to my amazing husband for supporting me throughout this journey of becoming a first-time author. To my children, this is a dream come true. Don't let anything stop you from being and becoming who God says you are.

To my amazing Heavenly Angel, my daughter Ja'Nasia Miller who inspired me and helped open my eyes: Thank you for being my mentor and for showing me how a mother is unconditional for a lifetime! Ja'Nasia, you taught me that even through hurt & pain, I could still find Godly purpose. You understood your assignment when God gave it to you, and for that, I am grateful. The Nasia Foundation will be a lifetime legacy in your honor.

To Ms. Cathy Harris, you are greatly appreciated, and thank you for not prematurely moving out of the Will of God; your No wasn't in Vain!!!

To Tucker Publishing House, your professionalism on this project was far beyond exceptional!!!

To my parents (biological & spiritually), your support is far beyond what I could ever imagine! Thank you for every prayer, encouraging word, and correction! To all the co-authors, thank you for inspiring me in ways you didn't know you had. May there continue to be blessings and peace upon each and every one on this project, and to my readers, thank you

Nadine Owens: I would like to acknowledge my daughter Tamara Pritchard for always supporting me; My sons Marcus

Pritchard, Tevin Owens, and Jeffery Owens for teaching me how to love unconditionally and never to give up. To my sister Serena Harris and Mr. Jeffrey Owens, thank you.

Nischelle Buffalow: I would like to thank Catherine Staton for asking me to be a co-author. I never would imagine myself being an author.

To my family and friends: Thank you for taking on this initiative to serve others. I don't know how I would have made it this far without you.

To my mother, Delena Buffalow, when I came to you 12 years ago, you said, "Go for it." You have been at my side and there through it all, making sacrifices to allow me to serve as God has called me to do. You are my superhero.

I thank everyone for their love, patience, support, and encouragement.

And I give God the glory, honor, and the praise for choosing me to serve others.

Ronjeanna Harris: I want to first give honor to my Lord Savior Jesus Christ!

My Husband Floyd, our amazing kids, and granddaughter!

My amazing parents, Deacon Ronnie & Minister Barbara Smith!

My Spiritual Parents Apostle & Apostle Elect Ducksworth!

My Mentors…

Thank you all so much for your support!

Tanikwa Matthews: Through the most challenging times in my life, I realized how much I had overcome. The climb to victory was a place I already owned, and I simply needed to walk in it. I want to acknowledge God, the Father, for life itself; without Him, I'm nothing but a mere vapor; with Him, I can do all things!

My boys, the greatest four gifts I've ever received: The Fantastic Four, my guys, my north, south, east, and west Tyrell Crockett, Jordan White, Jeremiah White, and Antoine White, I love you and thank God for each of you!

My parents, Bennie Matthews, and Drucilla Beach, I love you, and there's nothing you can do about it.

Grandmothers Julia Dickerson and Ella Matthews, Stepdad Joshua "Welt" Beach, Brothers Dominic, Josh, and Brandon, y'all push me, and I'm grateful!

Your love and support for my entire Restoration Outreach Healing Ministry family mean so much, a special shout out to my Pastor JoAnn McCrary!

My Bestie, Bonita Jackson, for always encouraging and remaining optimistic.

Accountability partner and Sister Letitia Council

The WAVERS of 2018: Martha Cotto, Brandy Peat, Natasha Rivera, Hannah Kelly, Kiera Washington, Shaun Bambaata, and James Lowe.

XVII Keys of Strength and HR Southside LBU roses to you!

THANK YOU to everyone who has supported, sown into WAVE, and encouraged me!

Veronica McMillian: There are a few people I want to thank for helping make my dreams come true. Cathy Harris, thank you for allowing a first-time writer to be on a project with you. If it were not for you, I would not have given writing a book a second thought. I want to think all my co-writer for being queens and sharing your story. I want to acknowledge my husband, Kenneth McMillian, for always being my number one supporter and always being there for me.

Lastly, I thank God for allowing me to see another day and giving me the grace to keep pushing when I just wanted to stop and say maybe next time, but the time was now, and I thank you, God, for such a time. As this! Oh, let me not forget Tara Tucker for your wordsmith abilities. You ROCK, girl!

INTRODUCTION

Because the world is counting on you! At some point in our lives, most people find themselves declaring, "I want to change the world." Everyone was put on this earth to help someone in some way. You were called to make your impact on the world. Though no one person has the capability to alter the world on their own, you do have the ability to make a positive difference every day. Spreading kindness, love, and empowerment over time is enjoyable and results in concrete change. By working together with your community to change lives one day at a time, your actions can have a meaningful impact.

Yes, the world is changing daily, and you yourself can help change it. You don't have to be a superhero or a social media icon to influence people and make a difference in this world. "Be the world's change you wish to see." Most of us have heard this quote and perhaps been influenced by it. It's a lovely sentiment that reminds us that everyone has the ability to make a difference. What you do now, whether it's working at a food bank, creating a nonprofit, or doing something you love and are passionate about, can have a long-term impact.

I believe in you, and you are needed to create real change in the world. Together we can make a difference that will last forever. If you're interested in making the world a better place, read on to discover how one person can change the world and what makes a nonprofit successful. The World is Counting on

You! Yes, you!!! The world needs you. Trust God and be a force of change.

Congratulations to each of the co-authors of the Forces of Change book anthology project for sharing their powerful, empowering stories of impact about the "why" behind their life-changing nonprofits. Their stories will inspire you to "do something" and create a life worth living that centers around helping others.

Cathy Harris

Visionary of Forces of Change "Transformational Non-profit Stories of Leaders Who Are Paving the Way for Others To Take Action."

WEBSITE: www.thecathystaton.org

EMAIL: thefireyourfearcoach@gmail.com

SOCIAL MEDIA: @thefireyourfearcoach

Cathy Harris brings with her over 20 years of leadership development experience. Cathy is a 4x best-selling author, Christian counselor, dynamic motivational speaker, philanthropist, and life and business coach. Managing a successful nonprofit and teaching cutting-edge life skill strategies join uncompromising integrity as the hallmarks of Cathy's service to help women recover. Cathy has a passion for telling her story, helping others tell their stories, and sharing the tools she uses to not only survive but thrive. Cathy is a domestic violence and sexual assault advocate who provides messages of hope, inspiration, humor and encourages people to find their voice and use life's stumbling blocks to rebuild their own lives. She is the CEO and founder of MyHelpMyHope Foundation, Inc., a 501c3 nonprofit organization that assists women and children in crisis situations. She is the CEO of Kingdom Coaching & Consulting, LLC., a company that provides affordable life coaching to those who want to reach their maximum potential in life and business. Through lived experiences and a bachelor's degree in Life Coaching, Cathy provides one-on-one coaching, group coaching, and custom presentations. She uses proven techniques to help people find fulfillment in their lives while doing what they love.

Cathy is the recipient of the Wavy TV Channel 10 Who Care Award, the ZETA Phi Beta Sorority, Inc. Finer Woman Award, Hampton Roads Gazeti Exemplar Award, ACHI Magazine Woman of the year Award, and the Garden of Hope Unity Award from Gethsemane Community Fellowship Church, among others. Cathy's work has been featured on many television stations such as The Hampton Roads Show, Wavy TV 10, WVEC News Channel 13, WTKR News Channel 3, Virginia This Morning, the Dr. Oz Show, and many more. Cathy has also been featured in publications such as the Virginia Pilot, and the New Journal and Guide, the Gazeti, and Tidewater Women, to name a few. The Obama administration and Oprah Winfrey selected the MyHelpMyHope Foundation as a changemaker. During her matriculation, Catherine has earned an AS in Psychology, BS in Christian Counseling, BS in Life Coaching & BS in Addiction & Recovery from Liberty University. Cathy is currently working on obtaining her master's degree in Clinical Mental Health Counseling.

FROM PAIN TO A NONPROFIT

My nonprofit was birth out of my pain. I am a survivor of domestic violence and sexual assault. God used my story for His Glory. In my healing and transformation, I realized that I did not want anyone else to go through what I went through. In praying for a way to help God gave me a vision for the MyHelpMyHope Foundation.

MyHelpMyHope Foundation is a leading domestic violence advocate and 501c3 nonprofit organization that brings awareness to domestic violence, sexual assault, and human sex trafficking. Our mission is to create a safe place and a life abuse-free for all through awareness, services, and training for lasting change in the communities we serve. We provide resources, education, training, goal/life coaching, shelter, food, school uniforms and grant the wishes of children for Christmas who reside in local domestic violence and homeless shelters, foster care, social services, and others. We believe that everyone has the right to a healthy relationship and to live abuse free.

As an advocate for these causes, I also discovered my gift of speaking and helping those affected by these traumas heal and walk in their purpose. I do not heal anyone. God heals. He uses me to assist. I have written self-help books, I speak, and I have started a life coaching consulting business to help those who are hurting and having a hard time pushing past their pain. I remember the spirit leading me to join the praise dance team one day at the church I was attending. The ladies were showing me the steps for one of our dances, and I blacked out. I did not pass out, but I was sort of in a trance. At that very moment was when the Holy Spirit gave me the name of my nonprofit. We were practicing to a song called "My Help" by Beverly Crawford. And I heard the spirit say, "Your ministry will be called MyHelpMyHope, and you will go out and help women recover and show them the love of Christ." He showed me that I would assist women in trauma situations who find it hard to move past domestic, sexual assault, and other traumas that are holding them back. Then I heard my name being called, and I came out of the trance.

Over the years, through my nonprofit and working with women, teens, and children, I learned that there are many people broken who were in abusive relationships or marriages or those who were molested and raped. There are many women and men who go through things, and they grow up or end up with a lot of emotional baggage, hurt, pain, and unforgiveness. They are walking around with unhealed wounds and unresolved issues that are stopping them from being who God wants them to be. I realized that I was born to be doing exactly what I was doing. I found myself coaching women and assisting them in their healing process from broken places.

This is where my life coaching skills come in and why I decided to start my life coaching business. Before I started life coaching, I did a lot of research. I wanted to perfect my craft and bring life coaching services under my nonprofit. I found a lot of information and certifications, but I didn't trust a lot of the stuff I saw. For example, how can someone be certified over a weekend or a few days in life coaching? Because I didn't trust a lot of the things that I saw, I decided to go a step further than a certification. I wanted to stand out, and I wanted my clients to know that I was very serious about assisting them, so I obtained a bachelor's degree in Life Coaching. You can google and do your research, but you will not find too many Life Coaches with a bachelor's degree in Life coaching. I had this desire to help people in a deep way. I felt led into the counseling field. My goal is to become a mental health professional counselor to be better equipped to help God's people. I am in school for my master's now.

We cannot lead from a broken place. Leading from a broken place stunts growth and being all that you can be. That's why I help women recover. I want them to be all that they can be. Little did I know the plans God had in store for me. When I think about how he strategically led me down the path of everything that has happened to me since I left my first abusive marriage, I am in tears! I was in a physical, mental, verbal, and financially abusive marriage. Domestic violence was a curse in my family. My grandmother was abused, my mom, aunts, and my sister was abused. God used me to break this generational curse. At the time of writing for this book, my nonprofit is 11 years old. God showed me visions of ways to assist families who needed the community the most.

When visiting shelters, I didn't like what I saw, so I prayed for ways to be able to assist the families in a huge way. I think this is where the counseling journey comes in. This is not to say that the shelters were not helping because they were. I just wanted to make a difference in other ways. Starting my nonprofit was easy, and I did it without money. The hard part came trying to thrive.

Anyone can start a nonprofit, but how are you going to sustain it and keep it running is the question. I already had cards stacked up against me because there is a stigma with it comes to domestic violence. We are supposed to sweep it under the rug and not talk about it. I found it hard in the early years of my nonprofit to thrive. It was hard to get donations, and I found myself using my own money to help the population we served. I paid out of pocket for hotel stays, food, clothing, bus tickets, toys, and so much more. When I did this, God always gave it back double. We assist families year around with emergency shelter, food, clothing, and other resources. We refer them to other community partners if we cannot assist them. I get very emotional when we cannot help a family due to funding.

My dream is to one day open a domestic violence shelter. Did you know that there are more dog shelters than shelters to assist those who want to leave abusive situations? The thought of this makes me sick. I get calls all the time from women who have reached out to shelters, and they are full, or the shelters cannot help them. We do our best to try to assist them, but there are times we cannot do anything. Even the resources we refer them to are unable to assist them sometimes. There are not enough shelters to assist people who want to get help or leave their abusers.

One of the most important things MyHelpMyHope Foundation does is bring awareness. We hold free community events where we bring together other community partners such as the shelters, commonwealth attorneys, the mayor, vice-mayor, or anyone that can help victims of domestic violence, sexual assault, and human sex trafficking. We provide resources and have open discussions about these causes that destroy lives. The mission is to let the community know that there is help available and where to go for help. We provide school uniforms for children living in shelters. So many other organizations were giving school supplies. I prayed for something different, and Operation School Uniform was birthed. School uniforms reduce school absenteeism, game aggression generated from colors being worn, reduce bullying generated from clothing as a status symbol, and foster a more business-like approach to academics. Do me a favor and close your eyes. Now, imagine being a child who was torn away from your home because your mother or father was getting abused. You were used to getting Christmas, but you are in a shelter this time, living with a friend, family, in a hotel, or maybe even on the street. But you don't understand what's going on. All you want is Santa to bring you the toy that you want. I saw this happen in shelters.

I wanted to do something to blow the families' minds, and I wanted to create lasting memories that they would never forget. This is where Operation Wish List comes from. We grant the wishes within reason for children. One time a child put they wanted a home for Christmas. I cried for days. One day I will be able to grant this kind of wish. This is my favorite program. It's not about just giving toys away. So many people do that, and it's okay. I wanted to make what we do different. We show the love of Christ through toys. For entrepreneurs who want to make a difference in the world, starting a nonprofit organization can be an unforgettable experience. Building a successful nonprofit necessitates a unique set of skills and abilities, but the process is not different from that of launching a small business. Understanding the advantages of founding a nonprofit organization rather than a traditional business might help you decide if this is the correct path for you. "We can, each of us, do our part in ending domestic violence, sexual assault, and human sex trafficking. But we won't reach our goal unless many more contribute to the effort."

I remember being overwhelmed by the lack of support when I first started my organization. I would be in tears during my first few events because none of my so-called friends and supporters were coming out to my events. None of the support went past a social media like, and that is not real support. Real support is action. I was sharing this frustration with a deaconess at my church, and I will never forget her advice. She told me to "Let it go." I didn't want to hear that, but it changed my life and how I would ever think about supporters and having any event. She told me to stop worrying about who shows up and who doesn't show up at my events and just to do what God tells me to do. She said my biggest support would come from God and strangers. And she was right.

Since then, it doesn't matter if one person shows up at my event or 50; I carry on as if it was God sitting in the audience. I have learned that quality is better than quantity and that purpose will always beat popularity. God had one more thing for me to deal with, and that was support from the church I attended. I could not understand why my church would not support my community efforts. This was something else that ate at me on the inside. I would hear and see my colleague's churches supporting them, but I couldn't figure it out. I sat at a table and did not know anyone during an event I attended. We spoke, sharing what we did and how we knew the event organizers. No one at the table knew anything about me. After the event, on my way to the restroom, a man who happened to be an apostle, who was one of the people sitting at my table, asked me if he could speak to me. After I came out of the restroom, he introduced himself and held my hands, and told me God told him to tell me something. Now I am not big on people coming up to you and telling you God told them to tell me something. Some people are false prophets. I must protect my anointing. He said,

"God told me to tell you to let it go. "Let go of thinking your church is going to support you." "They are not going to help you. Just keep doing His Will." As this man spoke, tears fell from my eyes like a waterfall. At that very moment, I knew this was not a false prophet that this was real because this man didn't know me. How could he know what was tearing me up on the inside? It was all God. Never listen to naysayers or anyone that says you cannot do anything. I consider myself and my non-profit/ministry a steppingstone as one journeys through life. I have a gift to help people inside out of God's way.

You can light up the world with your gifts, and you can inspire others to do the same. Whether you want to start a non-profit, a business, write a book, anything that you want to do, I want you never to give up. Here is my truth. At least once a week, I want to give up. I say every year I am not going to do Operation School Uniform or Operation Wish List. The donations just don't come in. But then I remember that God is my provider. He gave me the vision so that He would provide the provisions. And He does just that. He blows my mind every time. One way God blew my mind was when I got an email in June of 2016 from someone who works at the White House when Barack Obama was in office. The email stated this, "Dear Catherine, Congratulations! You are one of the nominees chosen to attend The United State of Women Summit on June 14th here in Washington, DC. I was blown away!!! That was not all!!!!! Out of the thousands of women invited, Michelle Obama and Oprah Winfrey chose some organizations as change-makers. My God-given organization MyHelpMyHope was chosen as a changemaker!!! I could not believe it!!!! God showed out! I don't do anything for recognition, accolades, or awards. I have received many awards for the work we do through my nonprofit, but this recognition was priceless!!! It was an amazing experience and I was just feet away from Oprah and Michelle. This was another way that God showed me that I was doing what he called me to do and I was doing it right! There are thousands of nonprofits all over the world big and small. I believe it's the smaller nonprofits that make the bigger impact. It's the smaller nonprofits that put boots to the ground and that are really making a difference in people's lives. I see this every day. Do it from the heart with pure intentions and watch what God will do. I often talk to God about my calling. Sometimes I feel like He gave me the hardest calling in the world. We all have those days where we don't want to get out of bed when we are tired of asking for help; we are just sick and tired of being sick and tired. When I feel like giving up, I sit and think about the "WHY." Two questions come to mind.

"Why did God bring me to this point" and "Why and I doing this." I am reminded that God did not bring me this far to give up. Going back to your "Why" brings you clarity. It allows you to revisit your goals, re-adjust and move forward. God did not do all that He did to change my life for me just to throw in the towel. But I am human, and I come close. My walk is not easy, and running a nonprofit is not easy. I get frustrated, and there are times when I feel like I am in this all by myself. But God always sends something or somebody my way to help me to keep going. What keeps me going is God. All of my help comes from Him.

Another thing that keeps me going is accepting the fact that some things will get tough. Everything will not be easy, and everything that I am going through is preparing me for what is coming. The feeling of giving up will come and go, but I have learned to be happy and persistent. Persistence and knowing God is with me every step of the way. God is with you. Whatever it is He is telling you to do, do it. Start that nonprofit and change the world! I am praying and cheering you on!

Inspired by a genuine desire to help others, Letitia Council, Founder and President of The Nasia Foundation, is a woman on a mission. She is a Traumatic Brain Injury & Caregiver Advocate who loves to share her story about her WHY? She encourages these women and assists them in rising from the ashes of their trauma. She has been blessed to be a part of many different organizations that support those

in need. Letitia is a Certified Nursing Assistant, Certified Life Coach, and has an Associate of Occupational Science Degree in Medical Assisting.

HOPELESS TO HOPEFUL

My name is Letitia Council. I am a Woman of God, Founder and President of The Nasia Foundation, motivational and inspirational speaker, author, wife, and mother, and I am wonderfully made. Being who I am today didn't come easy. My life journey to the road of success looked hopeless for a while. For the longest time, I wondered and questioned my purpose in life besides being my mother to my children and wife to my husband. I was working as a Certified Nursing Assistant. I believed it to be my long-term career field, helping the elderly who could no longer support themselves. I was fulfilling my passion, and my purpose was still vague. When my life took a turn in August 2019, my passion had faded, and my purpose was still unclear.

On the evening of August 15, 2019, our lives changed! That evening, I received a call back after just speaking to our oldest daughter about being safe on the highway. The call I received caused me to stop everything I was doing and run to my mother-in-law's vehicle and drive as fast and safely as I could to arrive at the scene of the accident where our daughter had survived a life-threatening accident!! When I saw my vehicle, there were no words to describe the feeling and emotion that came over me. My car looked like a Hi-C juice box once you suck in all the air. My daughter and the other young ladies survived that accident by the Grace of God!! My daughter wasn't on the scene when I arrived. She had already been transported to the hospital. Now

I have to be honest, when I arrived at the scene, I didn't recall asking for my daughter (my mind hadn't processed what my eyes were seeing). It was not until the officer informed me that all the ladies made it out alive that caused me to say, my daughter!!!! My cries became louder and louder. I was being coached to breathe (and told that?) God was with the girls.

I finally was able to get myself together enough to make a few phone calls. One call to my husband, the next call to my cousin, and I believe the last was to my supervisor, letting them know I would not be at work.

When I finally arrived at the Emergency room parking lot, I saw my husband, mother-in-law, and our youngest daughter. As I got out of the vehicle, I overheard one paramedic mention my daughter's last name. I spoke up and said, that is my daughter. He informed me that he needed some information and that she went unconscious on the ride and had to be placed on a ventilator. My heart sank to my feet! I got to registration in the ER department, told them who I was there for, and waited about five minutes for the trauma doctor to come out. He told me my daughter was on a ventilator, still unconscious, and her life-threatening injuries. When I walked into the room, my daughter was in. I cried more! I said, "Nasia, mommy is here with you, and I'm NOT going anywhere. I know you can hear me!"

Afterward, we walked from the emergency department to ICU (Intensive Care Unit), where Nasia proceeded to be hospitalized for ten days. While the nursing team was doing their assessment, my husband and I had to wait in the waiting area until the neurosurgeon came out to speak with us. We met him in the consultation room, where he then gave us news that NO parent is ever ready to receive. He explained her injuries to us, and that's when we learned that she had hit her head on the right frontal side and had excessive swelling and bleeding. The neurosurgeon explained to us that her injuries were life-threatening and that with his experience working with brain trauma, the patient's quality of life is nearly ending! He proceeded to say that even if he were to perform surgery, it would not even give her a fifty percent chance at life.

"So, you mean to tell me I need to call family?"

He replied, "I can't tell you what to do; I'm just giving you what I know from experience."

While we were in the room with the doctor, God was in there with Nasia! He was there all along! My husband exited the consultation room before me. When I walked out of that room and back into the waiting room, I sat down with tears rolling down my face, my cries aloud, and strangers began to pray for my family and me. At that moment, I surrendered ALL UNTO GOD! I believe in my heart when I surrendered unto Him; things began to turn around! While Nasia was still being assessed by the nurses, God was performing miracles! My husband and I had to get ourselves together before our other children arrived to visit their sister lying in a hospital bed on a ventilator fighting for her life. The tragedy we had to face and deal with was nothing short of a blessing and miracle from God!

On August 16, 2009, before the 7:00 am hour, the same doctor that told us Nasia's quality of life would soon come to an end was now saying, "I see some improvements that have taken place. Would you like for me to perform surgery?"

"Absolutely!"

What kind of mother would I be to say no, knowing my answer would give my daughter a second chance at life!" The doctor explained the surgery to my husband and me. He stated that he would remove her right frontal bone flap; with the removal, it will give the swelling flowing room. Once the swelling goes down, it will be a soft spot there, and she would have to wear a helmet when sitting up out of bed. Nasia had to get measurements for the helmet; the helmet was a soft firm-like helmet. Once her head was measured for her helmet, the doctor put the order in for it, and we had it when it was time to use it.

Once the major surgery was completed, we were told that she would need two more surgeries, one for a tracheotomy and the other for a G-tube. The tracheotomy would help with her breathing; before the Trach, she had an NG tube through her nose connected to the ventilator. The G-Tube was for nutrition.

On Nasia's tenth day in the hospital, she was no longer critical. She was in a medically induced coma but was stable enough to transfer out of ICU to a step-down unit. They would then focus on weaning her off the ventilator because she had started to breathe independently while doing breathing trials.

On day sixteen, she was completely off the ventilator! From day 16 to the 27th day, God was still performing Miracles. On day 26, Nasia sat up in a high back recliner chair for the first time. On day 28, she was released from the hospital and transferred to Sheltering Arms Rehabilitation in Richmond, VA. Doctors couldn't estimate how long Nasia would be in the hospital before going to the next level that would assist with her healing and Recovery. It was the day of September 12, 2019, that Nasia was being transported from Norfolk to Richmond. We drove down to Richmond to be right there by our warrior's bedside. Nasia's body had a spiked fever; your body needs to be cool when you have experienced a brain injury. Her body became overheated on the ride due to an air conditioning malfunction. The nursing staff was able to get her body temperature back down to normal.

The doctor at the rehab was phenomenal. He was knowledgeable of her current status, made some adjustments to her medication that would assist in awakening the brain more so the activity of the brain could be more stimulated. During her three-week stay, we saw more and more processes in Nasia's Recovery. She was released home in our care on October 3, 2019.

We were excited to have our daughter back home. Being surrounded by her loved ones played a big role in her Recovery. She came home with a Trach and feeding tube. While her mom did not know about caring for a Trach, she showed her willingness to learn the proper way to care for a Trach so that no infections would occur. Once mom learned to properly care for Nasia's Trach, the care became easy yet teachable each day. Her mother became her primary caregiver and immediately began to use her skills as a CNA to care for her daughter. Mom had to learn to give Trach and G- Tube care and administer medication via G-Tube. Although a skilled nurse had been assigned to Nasia, her mom continued to learn how to provide care on a nurse level. Once mom got that down packed, the nurse spoke with her supervisor to inform them her service wasn't needed. Mom was doing a great job. Nasia had a home health therapy team that also continued to play a big role in her recovery.

After a month of being home, Nasia became more alert and aware of her surroundings. She began to respond with head nods of yes and no. As she continued to process, she learned to cry and make faces. We loved every bit of the communication skills that she had developed. In November 2019, we celebrated our first Thanksgiving in our new life since the tragedy had occurred. We, as a family, celebrated every improvement that was taking place, no matter how small or big. Each accomplishment showed us, and we could overcome the smallest obstacle against us. God used Nasia to show us as a family that we could overcome any obstacle in our lives that is set out to destroy us, but instead of being destroyed, we pulled on God for strength and comfort. Our daughter knew that a celebration of Thanks was taking place, and it was nothing but love being shown.

One person sat across from Nasia, and when the individual called Nasia's name, Nasia's eyes were shocked; they could tell by the look in her eyes. That is when Angel knew that the brain injury only took away the movement of Nasia's limb, not her mind. Angel is a close cousin of Nasia. Angel began to talk to Nasia, and her eye contact showed that she was interested in what was being said. Something had transpired between the two. Nasia's eyes became watery to say. I know who you are. You came to visit me in the hospital; I heard your voice. I may not be the same, Nasia, but I am here, and I love you. Thank you for being here with me through it all. Angel became teary-eyed as well. Their connection made us realize even more that Nasia was becoming more cognitive. From that moment forth, Nasia's cognitive level began to improve.

In November 2020, Nasia received a trial basis communication device. The communication device gave us a general idea of how her eyesight was. We noticed some changes in her pupils, which showed us that something was going on with her vision. Admirably, she adapted to the device for the three days that we had it. Seeing her pupils change from brown to grey and her left eye not tracking as it should, I researched an eye doctor specializing in TBI (Traumatic Brain Injury).

To God be The Glory, we were able to not only find one, but the doctor also accepted her as a patient based on the intake form that we completed. When we had our first appointment, as all doctors do, they went over the patient's history to make sure nothing was missed. Upon the doctor assessing Nasia's eyes, he discovered that Nasia had fluid buildup in the eye coronal. We don't know how long the fluid had been there; in November, her appointment was made for January 2021. Nobody but God blocked the damage that the fluid could've caused, which was becoming blind in both eyes. We followed the doctors' orders once and were scheduled to see him again in April. On April 23, 2021, when we went back to the doctor and did his assessment, the fluid had decreased, but her eyes were still a little greyish.

On January 16, 2020, Nasia was scheduled to have her second Brain surgery, but because her bone flapped had not arrived at the hospital, her surgery was scheduled for the next day. On January

16, I received a text message asking me, have God mandated me to do something? My response was yes, "God and I had a conversation back in September about doing something for the youth, but what and how were my thoughts." After I replied to that text, God immediately gave me Nasia Foundation. Nasia Foundation was conceived in February 2020 with just a Facebook page; on April 27, 2020, Nasia Foundation was birthed amid a pandemic! Nasia Foundation is now a 501c3 nonprofit organization focused on Traumatic Brain Teen Survivors & caregivers where we "Live our Lives Through Their Minds." The Nasia foundation is different from other nonprofits that focus on an illness that changes lives.

As a nonprofit organization, we take the steps necessary to assist the caregiver in the home to properly care for their Traumatic Brain Injury, Teen or Young Adult. We provide training resources that will go into the house to meet the needs of both the survivor & caregiver, such as physical therapists, speech therapists, occupational therapists, and self-care strategists.

The Nasia Foundation doesn't just provide educational information; our Founder is on the journey alongside the families. The Nasia Foundation will be bridging the gap between returning home from rehab and assisting with beating the odds of Traumatic Brain Injury.

Our organization was started to raise Brain Injury Awareness and show how we can turn our hurt, pain & frustration into Hope, Purpose, and Impact.

Since operating the organization, I have met other mothers whom I may identify with on their journey. Most of the mother's live miles away from me, yet there is one close mother whom I admire her strength and her daughter's strength. We as mothers are already caregivers by nature; never in our minds would we think to become actual medical caregivers to our children who are fighting for their lives daily with Traumatic Brain Injury. While our children are fighting, we, too, are fighting

My life has profoundly changed due to the tragic accident that caused my child's engine (the brain) to become abnormal. For any mother experiencing that level of trauma, it is normal to step outside her comfort zone. Also, she doesn't mind being in uncomfortable positions for her child's strength that lay on the bed of affliction.

Helping other moms allowed me to identify with other things that come along with Traumatic Brain Injury if we hadn't already experienced it. I had one mom share with me the positive effects that Ambien had on her daughter. Yes, all medications affect us differently. I spoke with Nasia's doctor about doing an Ambien trial to see if we could see positive results. He agreed, and in a week, we saw positive results. Ambien is a medication used to treat depression and anxiety, but in Brain Injury survivors, it helps wake the brain stem up more, which causes you to have an increase of movement within your body. The conversations between myself and each mother made me realize that The Nasia Foundation's birthing season was right on time, GOD'S TIME! I just needed to Tap in! Nasia's Foundation provides a support system for mothers and their teens who have experienced the heart-wrenching Traumatic Brain Injury tragedy.

The Nasia foundation is different from other nonprofits that focus on an illness that changes lives. As a nonprofit organization, we take the steps necessary to assist the caregiver in the home to properly care for their Traumatic Brain Injury, Teen or Young Adult. We provide training resources that will go into the house to assist with meeting the needs of both the survivor & caregiver, such as a physical therapist, speech therapist, occupational therapist, self-care strategists, and our Founder! The Nasia Foundation doesn't just provide educational information; our Founder is on the journey alongside the families. The Nasia Foundation will be bridging the gap between returning home from rehab and assisting with beating the odds of Traumatic Brain Injury. We don't just want to be an organization that provides educational information and professional resources connections.

The Nasia Foundation provides direct contact services. We make weekly check-ins versus monthly support. We believe in going from strangers to the family throughout this journey. No one walks alone while navigating through Traumatic Brain Injury.

The Nasia Foundation has made an impact in the Traumatic Brain Injury Community and assisted and collaborated with other local nonprofits in providing hot meals, lunches, and snacks for our local community.

God gave us a second chance to love on Nasia. In all my praying, I prayed daily to hear my daughter's voice again. Every day while caring for her, I would ask her to "say, Mom." Nasia would shake her head no; her form of communication had increased over time. Nasia had begun making movements in her mouth. She would often form her mouth to say words, but no sound would come out. Nasia was a strong fighter. I would ask her, "You want something to drink?" she nodded her head yes or no, and when she nodded yes, I would give her sips of water or juice. She loved to taste the flavor, whether it be food or liquid. We had formed an 'I love you' communication pattern. I would say, "Nasia, you love mommy?" she would nod yes; "Nasia blink twice to say, you love daddy." She would. Nasia loved her siblings. She knew each of them by the mention of their names. Traumatic Brain Injury caused our lives to shift! As a family, we did not let that shift take us down! We fought with our Fighter!

On April 23, 2021, I did our nightly routine, gave care nightly medication, and prayed. After I was done praying, I went into my room and prepared for bed. When I got in my bed, I did not go straight to sleep that night. I was up on my phone; I heard a noise coming from Nasia. I got up and ran to her room. I motioned for my youngest daughter to go into Nasia's room with me; as we stood there and watched her mouth move and the sounds come out, excitement filled our hearts, I said thank you, Jesus, I ran back to my room to get my phone and began recording the sounds she was making. At that moment, God had manifested my prayers. Nasia had said "MOM"! I didn't realize she had said it until after my pastor said I played the recording over and over last night, and she said, MOM!!!! I went to replay the voice recording, and sure enough, NASIA SAID MOM!!!! The tears that fell from my face, God Thank You. That was the first time I had heard my baby say MOM in over a year!

The morning of April 25, 2021, I was standing in front of Nasia's tv, and a vision popped in my head, showing me that Nasia was about to pass.

I shook my head. "No, not my baby. God is not ready for her. Devil, leave me alone!"

That vision popped in my head twice. After shaking the image off the second time, I saw a funeral and myself and my husband standing over the casket. The person hadn't been revealed.

On my way to church, the same vision of us standing over a casket popped in my head again. The previous night God had dropped in my spirit that it would be a 911 call on Sunday morning. God showed me that my cell phone would be ringing, and it would be from my husband. I would answer, and my husband would say I need you to come back home. On my drive to church that Sunday morning, I saw the funeral again. Still, the person in the casket had not been revealed.

When I arrived at church, I was not in church for more than twenty minutes; my husband called and said, "I need for you to come back home!"

Apostle went to get my cousin. We walked out of the church to our vehicles, still with tears rolling down my face. When my cousin sat my phone on the armrest, I saw the paramedics pull our baby from her bed! I informed my apostle of the call with tears running down my face.

I said, "Lord, what is going on? Why are the paramedics at my house and pulling my baby out of bed?"

When I arrived home safely, my husband met me on our sidewalk. We walked into the house, and I saw our daughter lying on the floor receiving CPR. A guy from the paramedic team spoke with me, saying, "Ma'am? When we arrived, your daughter didn't have a pulse, we were able to get a faint one, but it didn't last long. We have been performing CPR for thirteen minutes, and we have to do twenty minutes of CPR."

Minutes later, I walked into our family room and stood next to another paramedic. He began to talk to me, and the only words I heard him say was "TERMINATION"! That is when reality hit that God had called Nasia home to rest in his arms. Nasia's death was unexpected, yet she prepared us to get ready. She had already got prepared. Nasia had gained her Heavenly Wings. She received her new body; she could not walk here on earth. In Heaven, she is walking around, dancing and laughing.

Although our hearts were not ready, her wings were. Nasia's purpose was to push me into my God-given purpose. Her assignment here on earth was complete, and God said, "Well done, my daughter."

Nasia Foundation shall continue to live on the legacy of Ja'Nasia as we continue to raise awareness, share our story, and impact the nation.

Our long-term goal is to have a fully operated group home for Traumatic Brain Injury in Teens & Young Adult survivors. The home will be set up to house twelve TBI survivors, have availability for six respite survivors and daycare operation.

These goals are extremely important to our organization because we want to be the change we have envisioned. Traumatic Brain Injury is an invisible disability, and The Nasia Foundation's goal is to help make the change to a visible disability.

While having the home for survivors, the curriculum activities within the home will consist of Home Redevelopment Learning Skills, Economic Redevelopment Skills, indoor & outdoor fun activities, wellness meals & snacks, and day trips.

I coach my way through with positive affirmations. Before my daughter passed, I didn't get the urge to give up much because I saw the purpose of my "WHY" daily. Nasia was well aware that we had founded a nonprofit organization with her name attached to it to raise awareness in the Traumatic Brain Injury Community. So, she was my push to keep going even when it became overwhelming.

When God called her home, and I took a break away from the organization, thoughts would run through my mind. "I know I got to keep the foundation going," I don't feel like it, what's the purpose?" but then I heard Nasia say, "Mommy, you can't stop the Traumatic Brain Injury Community still needs you; they need to know the challenges that we faced and how we overcame each obstacle. I'm still the purpose behind our 'WHY," so mommy, you can't give up!"

On the day our Nasia gained her heavenly wings, I received a visit from another mother who has been on the journey of Traumatic Brain Injury since 2018. She said to me, "You have made a huge IMPACT in our lives, as well as other lives that haven't even experienced Traumatic Brain Injury through your strength & inspiration!"

So, each time my flesh wants to give up, God speaks, and Nasia speaks to remind me of the IMPACT I made! No matter how difficult I find some days to be, pushing forward with The Nasia Foundation, I WON' T FORFEIT!

I did not make it this far to turn back to my ugly and ungodly ways. I was out in left field for a long time. (Btw I used to love playing in left field when I played softball in high school center & left were the only two positions I played). But in life outside the softball field, my left field was completely different. I would compromise my identity by being like those I associated myself with; I did that for many years, yes, even as a single mother n then wife! I was overcome by Testimony; God had a plan that worked better for my good! Trust God: His plan is better and much greater than ours.

Jeremiah 30:17(KJV)-For I will restore health unto thee, and I will heal thee of thy wounds, saith the Lord; because they called thee an Outcast, saying, This is Zion, whom no man seeketh after.

Our Mission here at The Nasia Foundation is to provide a support system for mothers and their teens who have experienced the heart-wrenching tragedy of Traumatic Brain Injury.

Nasia's Foundation aims to provide not only emotional support but financial support to aid in times of uncertainty. Nasia's Foundation strives to bring TBI awareness to disabled teens in our community to help moms strive and thrive through their journey of TBI. Our resources help stabilize families devastated by TBI. By reducing stigma, we equip families to lead secure lives with greater levels of functionality. This improves the quality of life for caretakers and enhances the life experiences of TBI survivors.

The Nasia Foundation programs are:

- Caregiver Care kits to help implement self-care. As caregivers, we don't take enough time out for ourselves; we can't continue to pour from an empty cup. As experienced caregivers, it's very important to replenish ourselves.
- Traumatic Brain Injury Survivors Care Kits: it's the thought of being thought of by others who understand the needs of the survivors. Since we began the Care Kit program for Traumatic Brain Injury Teen & Young adults and caregivers, it has shown families that they are cared for and always thought of. It has reminded the caregiver to take time for themselves without regrets. So far, we have provided kits to four families locally and out of state.
- Caregiver & Traumatic Brain Injury support group; just to connect with others who have also endured the challenges that someone is affected by with TBI.
- Resource connections: One can't do it alone; having information at a family's fingertip helps with stress levels.

Monetary Donations goes towards the following services that The Nasia Foundation provides:

Traumatic Brain Injury Conferences & Webinar to continue raising awareness to those who may not know about TBI and to bring more education to the TBI community. College Scholarship Funding to high school seniors whose career choice is in the medical field and Traumatic Brain Injury Advocacy for those unable to speak and advocate for themselves. Life & Recovery Coaching to assist with overcoming the trauma that one has endured.

I'm a native of the beautiful Eastern Shore, Virginia. I received my education from Accomack County Public Schools. In 2005 I decided to transition to the Hampton Roads area because I wanted a better life for myself and my two children. In 2008 I met my NOW husband and completed my associate degree program as a Medical Assistant. In 2010 our family grew from six to a family of seven!

I am now a DAUGHTER of THE KING, the Founder, and President of a 501c3 nonprofit organization, author, Life & Recovery Coach, Inspirational Speaker, business partner! I am not who I didn't believe I could become; I AM EVERYTHING GOD SAY I AM!

Never give up on your dreams and passion! If you believe that you have what it takes to start a nonprofit organization,

- Put in the time to align yourself with successful nonprofit founders,
- Ask them to become your mentor.
- Become a volunteer with an organization that is like your passion and receive the guidance you need before starting.
- Write your vision down and make it plan.
- Begin with a business plan, pray, and ask God for the name of your business,

- Create your mission and vision statement.

- Create your content for your organization.

- Do the research to get assistance with registration within the state you live in.

- Don't start a nonprofit cause your friend started one; running a successful 501c3 organization is hard work, and it requires long hours, dedication, and perseverance! If you believe in yourself, GO FORTH!

Words of Encouragement

Never let what someone is doing Hinder you. Pray to ask God to release your past so that it does not Hinder you. Your past does not define your future.

"Living Their Lives Through Our Minds."

www.thenasiafoundation.org

Nadine-Pritchard Owens is the CEO of Our Brother's Keeper Inc. (OBK). Nadine has been a caregiver and parent advocate for more than 20 years to her adult sons with different abilities. She knows first-hand the challenges, the struggles, and the emotional rollercoaster that goes hand to hand with pouring out so much. Nadine is a certified Life Coach,  financial advisor, administrator, author, and the owner of Our Brother's Keeper Homecare.

Nadine consults with women, men, and people with different abilities. Nadine heads up a feeding program to feed as many people as possible. She also trains parents in handling stress in a healthy manner.

Nadine believes in the biblical principles which shaped and formed her into the woman she is today. She holds a wealth of knowledge and wisdom regarding various areas of independence, self-care, and dignity. She has a passion for assisting the needs of others, including caregivers, parents, and people in the healthcare field. Nadine also speaks at different events, volunteers her services to fight for insurance, equal rights, equal pay, and quality care for health insurance. Nadine is also a certified emotional intelligence coach. She believes in growing yourself, which she is advancing her studies at Tidewater Community College (TCC). Nadine desires to spread the importance of loving yourself to the fullest.

OUR BROTHER'S KEEPER

For as long as I can remember, I was always a giver and helper to anyone in need. So, it was already instilled in me even at a young age.

My name is Nadine Owens, and I am a certified life coach, international motivational speaker, author, entrepreneur, and caregiver to my adult sons with autism. Life has not always been easy. I am a mother of five, two girls and three boys. My boys have autism, and raising my sons was not easy. I suffered from depression, anxiety, low self-esteem, isolation, and wanting to give up. Nothing changed for me until I decided I wanted to live and not die. I changed what I was eating and what was eating me. I started to give to myself first until my cup ran over, then I gave from my overflow. I started to fuel my mind with affirmations, and meditations, my body with sleep, exercise, and water, my spirit with prayer and the word of God. Once I started working on myself, I became an advocate and made one of my missions to help every parent, caregiver, and person with different abilities be the best version of themselves. By changing their mind, they can change their life. I always wanted to start a resource center to connect people with the resources they need and give parents, caregivers, and people with different abilities hope. Every time I began the process of finding a building, I let fear, intimidation, lack of knowledge, money, not knowing the right people, and not having the resources myself stop me! The Lord told me five times to start a resource center.

The sixth time He used my daughter. One day my daughter came to me with a notebook in her hand and asked me if she could talk to me. She said that she wanted to start a t-shirt business. "Tamara, OK! You never done a t-shirt a day in your life."

You see, my daughter had just finished her bachelor's and was going back to Regent University to get her Master's in two weeks. I asked her what made her want to start a t-shirt business. She said she woke up and wrote down everything given to her by God. After she finished talking, I turned around, and the Lord said, "That's her vision, not yours!" I immediately turned around and said, "You know I'm team, Tamara." I just wanted to make sure I got revenue in return because I knew she wanted a loan. She showed me her business plan, and I was very impressed.

A few days passed, and I was looking at the television, and the Lord said, "Get a building." I looked around and immediately grabbed the phone to call Tamara. This was on a Sunday at 6:55 in the morning.

"Tamara, have you been looking for a building?"

"Yes, ma'am," she replied.

"Why didn't you tell me?"

You didn't give me a chance to."

"You need to call them."

"Today?"

I answered, "Yes, you do not understand."

As time went on, I didn't hear from her. Then early Monday morning, I gave Tamara a call and asked her if she could call to find out if any buildings were available?

"No, because some friends came over, and I had a cookout."

"Tamara, you need to call now!"

"OK."

Tamara called me back within 5 minutes and said one of the building owners said they would be in town to show her the building in two days. She asked me if I would go with her to see the building and I said absolutely! I met Tamara at the location. Tamara and I got out of the car at the same time the landlord walked over to Tamara and gave her the keys. She looked at me; I said, "Let's go see the building."

When we got inside, it was two sides to the building. I said, "Tamera, you can you be on one side, and I can be on the other." *Fret, not small beginnings.*

That was the birth of Our Brother's Keeper. I started Our Brother's Keeper because I wanted to help as many families as I could connect to the best resources possible. I also wanted to help people with different abilities be included in an inclusive environment and to remain home or have their apartment with personal assistance to keep them out of group homes, nursing homes, and mental hospitals.

As a mom with adult sons with autism, I know how important it is to be educated and be connected to the right resources for your loved one. Not only do Our Brother's Keeper provide consultations, resources, advocacy, and education, but we also feed the community once a month, providing food to the homeless, elderly, low-income, and people with different abilities and their families.

Our Brother's Keeper also partners with other organizations to help with events, donate food, money, or volunteer our services to serve more people in the community. I think it is so important that nonprofits collaborate to serve more people in the community in a big and impactful way! I know firsthand that being a mom, entrepreneur, and caregiver can be quite challenging. I know the pain, setbacks, anxiety, depression, and fears that come alongside being a caregiver. I have helped families of people with different abilities by sharing my story and everything I have gone through. I tell them how I grew through it all so that I leave them with hope. I am the voice of hope, and I am on a mission to help as many families as I can.

How I started my nonprofit was not an easy process. Getting my 501C3 was very pricey, and I also had a building. Often when people start a nonprofit, they start from their house for a couple of years and then get a building. For me, I had a building since day one. So that means I already had overhead expenses that I had to pay on top of other utilities and bills that came with having a building. I also had to market, have a website, buy materials, supplies, etc. When starting my nonprofit, I could have saved a lot of money by doing some paperwork myself. I could have asked volunteers to help in other areas that I didn't have to pay other people to do.

I would like to give you some advice on starting a non-profit. But first, I will say, starting a nonprofit is not easy. This is not to scare you, stop you, or deter you from pursuing your dreams, but to inform you truthfully and prepare you for what's to come. Having a nonprofit takes time, energy, dedication, preparedness, sleepless nights, commitment, tough skin, faith, and wisdom.

Now with that being said, I didn't say it was impossible. People have different motives and agendas. All things are possible to them that believe. The question is, do you believe? I am going to give you the 10-step formula for starting a nonprofit. First, I want to say that please know or get to know the people that labor among you. As leaders, it's our job to distinguish the ones in your organization for the cause or the mission and those in your organization for themselves.

1. **Decide if you want a nonprofit or for-profit.** A non-profit is to fulfill a need in the community. You can earn a salary from your nonprofit.

2. **Be clear and concise about your purpose.** Study everything about your purpose. Study everything about your organization. Write down what your nonprofit will target. Write all your plans and thoughts about how you will fill that need. You will have to plan accordingly to raise money and work with boards of directors and volunteers to fulfill your purpose. Make sure you set aside time.

3. **Do your research.** Find out what organizations are doing the same thing as you so you will not be doing the same thing. You can adjust some things or take away something.

You have to look at the bigger picture. Your nonprofit will compete with donors, sponsors, charities, grants to stay in business (oh yea! Nonprofits are a business). You must fulfill a significant need that other organizations aren't already meeting. Research data to see how many people would benefit from your nonprofit.

Also, when researching, there are several questions you should consider:

1. **What problem or issues are you looking to solve?**
   a. You should be as direct as possible when addressing the issue. By establishing your niche, your chances of intersecting with other organizations decreases.
2. **How many organizations address the same issue?**
   b. The reason organizations exist is to solve a common issue. Every organization is unique, whether it has a strong network of trained staff, difficult strategies for solving problems, or advocating and educating, bringing awareness. (How many people out there want to see their problems addressed? So many would like to see change. Are there ways you can make them interested?

   With starting anything, there must be an interest in what you are offering. However, sometimes people don't know what is available until you show them. So, suppose there is no significant demand for what your nonprofit offers. In that case, you should have a plan to make them interested.

Do you have the resources, connections, and plan to operate a functional nonprofit? If not, where would you get the resources? How long will it take before your nonprofit is fully operating?

Upon answering these questions, you should have a decent idea about the viability of your nonprofit and your pitch and strategies of how to market, but also make sure you have all the logistics.

4. **Apply for your 501C3 status-** Either you can file the paperwork yourself, or you can hire someone to do all the paperwork for your nonprofit needs. First, you could get legal advice from a lawyer or an accountant who has experience with nonprofits. You can always get someone to answer your questions, prepare and review your application to help you gain internal revenue service approval, and avoid problems down the road.

There are unique tax laws to abide by and failing to make yourself familiar with these laws can and will cost you your status, so learn your federal government laws for each state. The IRS has plenty of guides on applying and maintaining your nonprofit status. Each state has its own rules, so you must research your state.

5. **State Tax Exemption-** After the IRS approves your nonprofit status, you can qualify for a state tax exemption. It depends on what state you are in and if you have to apply for it separately.

6. **Form a nonprofit corporation-** You should create your nonprofit bylaws

Before applying for nonprofit tax status, you must form a nonprofit corporation. Creating a nonprofit involves filling paperwork with your state and paying filling fees.

7. **Fundraising Plan**- Make a concrete, realistic plan on how your organization will raise money. Fundraising is the cornerstone of any nonprofit organization. Develop your fundraising plan. Your fundraising plan will determine the future of your programs, your expansions, and how prospective donors will view you in terms of credibility. Consider investing in fundraiser software to jumpstart the process. The fundraising authority has developed a solid, replicable framework:

   a. The goal- Where do you see yourself in 5 years? Always begin with the end in mind. What will be your fundraising goals? More research will have to be done to determine the estimated costs of services programs, budget costs, infrastructure, and organization to determine this number.

   b. Your message is just like your business plan. Your fundraising plan should include a declaration of what you intend to do with the money earned/raised, what your message is, and your operating budget.

   c. The tactics- Knowing what is needed and what it will go towards. It is time to plan the methods you will use to raise the money now and in the future:

      1. Direct mail

      2. Crowd funding

      3. Grants

      4.   Major Donors

      5.   Fundraising

8. **Write a nonprofit business plan**- Once you plan, prepare. You are ready to write your business plan. Your business plan should include:

    a.   The need you will fill and how you will be different from each other.

    b.   A budget plan for a startup cost for running your nonprofit.

    c.   Questions? How do you raise funds? How will you get the money for your expenses?

    d.   Who will your board members be, which person will have certain positions, will you have paid staff, how many volunteers will you need?

    e.   How will you market your nonprofit? How will you attract donors? What will be your follow-up for donors and sponsors? How will you get the word out about your nonprofit?

       The business plan or strategic plan is one of the most important steps to starting a nonprofit. Because it helps you see the weaknesses in your ideas and strengths, it also provides you with a roadmap for your next steps and gives you all the information you need when applying for your nonprofit status.

    f.   Executive Summary- A clear overview of the business plan, including your mission, unique assets, programs, and financial proposals. This form is to let your donors and sponsors know what to reference.

g.   Organizational structure- Not only do others have to know what your organization intends to do, but they also need to know how it is run. Be sure to include written descriptions: products, programs, services. Be sure to mention all programs and have a break-down of what you will offer for the money that is being given to your organization. Make sure you list all functions and operations.

h.   Marketing plan- How will you market your organization, products, and services?

i.   Operational Plan- How will your offering be deliv-ered? Where will your programs be located? What access do you currently have to deliver on these pro-grams and services?

j.   Managements and operations team- Who do you have on the programs, and who are the leaders and other positions on these programs?

k.   Financial planning- What finances do you have? How much do you need to operate fully? Where do you plan on obtaining funding?

l.   Appendix- This is where you will put your staff resumes, documents, charts, graphics, all materials, and your annual reports once available.

m.   Your business plan should be updated along with the changes in your nonprofit outlook and goals.

9.   **Know your organization's impact**- By knowing what your organization is about, is one of the best ways to keep your team informed, to keep support flowing into

your organization, also to show the impact in terms of how many people you reached out to or served and how the money was spent. Have a system for measuring your nonprofit's impact starting from day one, and then you will be able to show data when you apply for grants or launch a fundraiser. Running a nonprofit business can be extremely rewarding and make a major difference in your community. Not only make sure you are filling your paperwork, make you are planning, researching, studying, asking questions, and staying focused. You will be achieving your goals and running a successful nonprofit.

10. **Having surveys**- By doing surveys, you will be able to get feedback from the community and the people you serve, and other nonprofits that do similar work. Find out the need and how the need can be met. See what's working and what's not working and create a plan of action for change.

Having a nonprofit can be challenging and very rewarding at the same time if you stay true to who you are, your mission, vision, and most importantly, your WHY; it is what motivates you, drives you, and keeps you focused. The reason why you are helping so many people is much bigger than us. If you keep that in mind, your organization will go further and grow. Do the work, the research, and ask the questions. Ask for help when you need it. My organization has support groups, events, training, and other things.

What sets my nonprofit apart is the love, compassion, and commitment I have for each parent, caregiver, and people with different abilities. I know firsthand how they feel, the struggles they go through, the frustration, not knowing the right questions to ask, or how to advocate for yourself. At Our Brothers Keeper, we do consultations and connect them with appropriate organizations and the right company that will help their needs.

One young mother that did not know who to turn to was so depressed she could barely function. Someone had given her my contact information, and she had contacted me. I told her my story and inspired her to increase her hope, and she felt better. She reached out for more help for herself and her loved ones. I am the voice of hope, and I want to help every woman not only exist but live and live life to the fullest! It gives me joy and satisfaction when helping other people. I also speak around the world to give women hope.

Finding balance for me is very important. Without balance, nothing will be done, and it will be very chaotic in my life and business. In order to be the best version of yourself, you have to give to yourself first until your cup runneth over, and you give from your overflow! I make sure that I give to myself mentally, physically, and spiritually. Mental by looking at motivational videos and saying affirmations every day builds me up and strengthens my core. I also exercise three times a week. I also drink six glasses of water at night to be refreshed in the morning. I also rest 6 to 8 hours for my spirit. I pray every day and read my word. I also have an attitude of gratitude. Once I apply these three steps every day, my day is ready to start. My sons have personal aides that help them in the morning with their ADL, which helps them get their day started. My sons attend Our Brother's Keeper Resource Center, where they receive training, education, motivation so they can live the best quality of life possible. I also make sure I spend quality time with my daughters by talking on the phone, going out to lunch, or just by talking to each other regularly. I am here for all of my children. It does not matter how old you are. You will always need your mother or someone to encourage you or pour into you. You are more than enough. Those words speak volumes! I want my girls to know who they are and whom they belong to.

My two daughters have kids as well. My oldest daughter Tamara has four children one daughter and three sons: Khliyia, Renardo, Kyrie, and Messiah. My youngest daughter Brianna has two children, one daughter and one son: Bella and Kayden. This is why it's so important that I keep everything balanced spending time with my grandkids and family are priceless. I also ask for help. It was hard for me to ask people because no one was there when I did reach out. Now I know who to reach out to and who not to reach out to. Ask for help, not because you are weak but because you want to remain strong.

In the beginning, things were hard, and it seemed like I was running into a brick wall. I wanted to say that I give up and that this is too much, but every time I felt like giving up, I looked at my boys, and they gave me the courage and strength to keep going. Talking to people and hearing their stories, testimonies, concerns, and their hopes for the future is what keeps me going. I love people, and I love helping people in a way that puts a smile on their face

All donations that come into Our Brothers Keeper are used for events, materials, hunger, and wellness programs that we feed the community once a month, and supplies needed for giveaways. All donations are tax-deductible.

If you would like to connect with me, book me for a speaking engagement or donate to Our Brothers' Keeper; here are the ways that you can do so:

www.ourbrotherskeeper.org
Facebook: our brother's keeper
Instagram: ourbrotherskeeper

Community advocate, and CEO of Buffalow Family and Friends Community Days, Nischelle Buffalow, was born in Chesapeake, Virginia, in 1971. She graduated from Indian River High School in 1989 and attended Norfolk State University, studying Accounting. Ms. Buffalow worked for the City of Chesapeake, Library Department, 1992-2012. From 2012 to now, Ms. Buffalow has served her community with educational, health, food, and essential daily resources. She is past Vice President of the South Norfolk Neighborhood Watch, past treasurer of the South Norfolk Neighborhood Watch, past secretary of the South Norfolk Revitalization Commission, past Board Member of Southeastern Virginia Homeless Coalition, and served on a Task force for Homelessness in the City of Chesapeake. 2015 Silver Star Spirit of Service Award from Urban League of Hampton Roads, 2017 Woman of the Year for the Women's Division of Hampton Roads Chamber of Commerce Chesapeake. 2018 State of Virginia Proclamation, 2016 and 2020 Citizen of the Year from Omega Psi Phi Fraternity Sigma Kappa Kappa Chapter.

BUFFALOW FAMILY AND FRIENDS

As a life-long practicing Christian, servant leadership came naturally to me. The scripture that provides the backbone of my servant leadership approach says: "In everything I have shown you that, by working hard, we must help the weak. In this way we remember the Lord Jesus' words: 'It is more blessed to give than to receive.'" (Acts 20:35 NIV)

A servant leader focuses on the organization's impact on its people and their community rather than on the organization itself. This is a vastly different leadership style with ten widely recognized characteristics that I try hard to use in guiding Buffalow Family and Friends Community Days. They are listening, empathy, healing, awareness, persuasion, conceptualization, foresight, stewardship, commitment to the growth of people, and building community. I try to use these skills with my Board, my volunteers, funders, and most importantly, the people we serve.

While the church played a key role in developing my core principles, so did my home life. Helping others was instilled in me at an early age. Because my mother was active military, as a child, I lived with my grandparents. My grandfather worked for a trucking company and took exceptionally good care of our family; my grandmother, uncle, and me. When my grandfather suffered a stroke in the late '70s, I matured quickly. I had to assist my grandmother with cooking and taking care of our home. Even though I was only in the third grade, I instantly became a caretaker for my grandmother once my grandfather died. Because she battled heart disease and gout, there were times my grandmother could not get out of bed and needed my assistance around our home. I watched my grandmother cook daily, and when she could not cook, sometimes, I would cook breakfast and other meals. When neighbors asked for a cup of sugar or a few eggs, I would give them what they needed. I continued my grandmother's practice of assisting the community.

I learned to catch public transportation to get money orders to pay our household bills. In addition, if there were enough funds left in the bank, I would sometimes buy my grandmother's medication. I saw firsthand how seniors battle to pay bills, have nutritious food, or purchase medication. This background with my grandparents, living in low-income housing in Chesapeake, personally experiencing having been without health insurance and struggling to get the necessary medicine has influenced the development of the programs we provide and impacted my empathy with the clients we serve.

In addition to teaching me about coping with life's struggles, my grandmother also taught me about serving others in small but meaningful ways. For example, she enjoyed cooking, and I would watch her in the kitchen cooking large meals, even though we had a small family. The extra food would be given to anyone that would knock on the door and ask for a meal, or she would have me take it to anyone who needed it. While we did not have a lot, what we had, my grandmother shared with others in need. She used her giving of food as the lesson that instilled the belief that we could be ordinary people working to make a difference in the lives of others. This became our mantra once Buffalow Family and Friends Community Days was established in November 2010.

In the early days of our operations, I pondered the thought of becoming a recognized nonprofit for years but worried that if I became a 501(c)3, my mission to serve would be hindered due to the regulations. However, after talking with a core group of knowledgeable individuals in 2012, I applied to the State Commission for the corporate charter. Then in 2014, I applied to the IRS for nonprofit status, and by January 2015, we became a fully recognized nonprofit organization established to serve Chesapeake, Virginia.

But all was not rosy just because I had my official documentation in order. We operated out of my home for years due to the lack of funding and knowledge on how to get funding. We could not afford to pay anyone for any type of work. I was glad to have an accounting background to manage funds and file a yearly tax return for the nonprofit. I depended on family and friends to purchase food and essential items to serve because our donation drives never pulled in enough supplies. Frankly, I thought once we became a nonprofit, it would be easy to get donations and grants; it was not.

Beyond our newness, lack-of-proven grant management, and experienced grant writers, the first challenge was that grant funding for purchasing food was not around in 2010. I would go to different meetings to gain and share information. Unfortunately, I learned that not only was there no funding available, but if I shared my story, mission, and dream, it might and even did, get taken from me by another group before I could initiate the plan. This happened because they had the resources I did not have.

I continued being grounded and worked hard to build the organization, and in May 2012, I took the leap of faith and quit my full-time job to minister my dream of serving others. Working in the city for 20 years, my last three years of employment felt like something was missing; it was my passion for helping others. I knew I would have to leave my job as a city employee to serve the communities. I asked the Lord how I would survive with no income, and in Proverbs 3:5-6 NIV, it says, "Trust in the Lord with all your heart and lean not on your own understanding; in all your ways submit to him, and he will make your paths straight."

Once my Uncle Earl was killed in a single-vehicle accident in Oklahoma, it really dawned on me that I needed to pursue my passion. I would always tell my Uncle Earl, who was very business-oriented, to invest his knowledge and energy into opening up his own company. A week before he died, he decided to do just that.

I realized God had a plan for me to be a servant. I began walking the grounds one community at a time and building relationships with individuals. This was critical! Because once those relationships were established, they would allow me in to serve them. Having built this trust, our senior communities depend on us and look to us for resources and voice their concerns.

Financial and Operational Support

In 2017, we were excited to receive our first grant to get supplies for one of our feeding initiatives. Unfortunately, while the grant could support the supplies needed for the program, it did not permit purchasing food, which was the most expensive critical item needed. We learned an important lesson in grant writing: the devil is in the details. However, with this initial funding success, we were able to seek other funders. In 2018, I submitted a grant to become a Community Food Hub that supports the city's vulnerable, homeless, families, and senior population. The Community Food Hub Grant has been awarded to us for the past three years, and we are grateful.

During the pandemic, grant money was available for organizations like Buffalow Family and Friends that feed the community. We received four grants to support food insecurities in communities. While we have been fortunate over the past few years, applying for and managing grants is challenging and time-consuming. Researching, writing, submitting, and then getting the notification that you did not receive the grant is a real blow for small organizations. Our eventual hope is not to have to rely on the unpredictability of grant funding and secure a designated line item from the city or another funder, but meanwhile, it and local donations remain our operating resource.

Why We Serve

Our primary goal is to minimize food insecurities within our communities and distribute clothing and daily essentials to individuals, families, and seniors in need. Many of the people we serve live in a food desert, meaning more than two miles to the closest grocery store. I have sat on my porch watching children and adults go to the local convenience store to get unhealthy food because they could not get anything else to eat. Many of them are elderly and have to rely on public transportation to get to that store, so their only other option is to use the closest convenience store to get canned and non-perishables. Many in my community also live on very fixed incomes and struggle to meet housing, food, and medical costs. Unfortunately, our city has limited programs to support them, and other agencies can't meet the need. After witnessing this continuing struggle amongst my neighbors, I was called to help.

How We Serve

Our annual Thanksgiving Day event is one of our early and ongoing efforts to address food and clothing challenges. Remembering the lessons from my Grandmother, sitting down with my mother, I asked if she would help me cook a Thanksgiving Meal to be served at the park. She said yes, and we recruited other family members and friends. This was November 2010.

With their assistance, food was purchased for our Thanksgiving Community Dinner. We stayed up late in the night, making a homemade meal to feed the homeless and the needy. My small team helped peel potatoes for sweet potato pies, white potatoes for mashed potatoes, ham, turkeys, and other fixings to serve. A few community people came out with items to serve.

We served around thirty people at a park near my home the first year. One gentleman joined us for dinner and shared that this was the first Thanksgiving without his father. He shared that he was so thankful for the meal and the company. It was just him and his father for many years, and they would eat together. Our meal assisted him with his grief, and he stayed and enjoyed the meal and others for many hours.

From that first meal in 2010, our Thanksgiving Dinner annual feeding has grown from feeding thirty people to 2,021 meals served in 2020 (despite Covid challenges). BFF community volunteers now include local and state politicians and many other community leaders and civic organizations volunteering to serve meals, make deserts, fry turkeys, grill hams, and deliver meals all over the city. Local students come out as well to volunteer to serve.

We realized that many elderly community members were shut-ins who needed meals on Thanksgiving Day by the third year. To reach the senior communities, we listed Thanksgiving Feeding in the local Clipper newspaper, walked flyers through senior communities, posted information on the Chesapeake TV Channel, and conducted outreach to area churches.

To handle the increased number of people being served, friends and volunteers turned the empty lot beside my house into an outdoor cooking space with turkey fryers, grills, tents, tables, and chairs. Tents were set up for a delivery section and for people walking up to eat. Some people would stay and socialize; others would take their meals home. Also, in year three, we asked people to donate gently used clothing, toiletries, and blankets so those in need could choose what they needed.

During the program's growth, we have consistently seen an increase in the number of volunteers and donors to the effort.

The local hospital has become the sponsor of the turkeys, and other agencies help secure other food items. Also increasing each year is the visibility of the program and the engagement by local officials. I sent letters to the City Council inviting them to the event, and one member came out the first year. A few years later, another city council member came out. It's taken many years of continuing our program development, but now city, state, and even federal officials have come out to support the mission.

Continuing to Figure Out

Buffalow Family and Friends feeding initiative started by ensuring everyone had a meal, especially on the holidays, but we knew this wasn't enough to meet the bigger needs. Over time we developed a broader vision to expand our outreach and increase our services. However, many challenges had to be addressed before taking the next step. The challenges to growing our food insecurity program included figuring out how to logistically bring in, store and distribute larger quantities of foods.

Our vehicle was traded for a larger one, our backyard was fenced, deep freezers and storage buildings were added, and every room in my house was used for BFF supplies. BFF and a few donors personally financed most of the cost, and my mother retired to help expand our workforce.

Our first major support for increasing our volume came when we started collaborating with the Foodbank of Southeast Virginia. This new Foodbank collaboration expanded our ability to get fresh produce, fruits, and protein into the community. We also developed a food rescue program with a local university and the Rotary. Winter, Spring, and Summer break, we were able to pick up food from Old Dominion University Food Services. They would also deliver fresh produce for us to hand out into the community, and the Rotary would share their monthly meeting foods for us to use with our feeding program.

Honestly, I seldom looked at the financial aspect of the initiative. I just knew we had to make sure everyone received healthy foods and meals. Sometimes I wondered, how are we going to feed for this outreach with little donations coming in. However, no outreach has been canceled due to a lack of funding. We always made it. I may get a lot of "Nos" when requesting funding and donations; however, I keep walking the ground until we can get a "Yes."

In 2020 we were blessed with two donated vehicles. In 2021, after several years of the successful partnership, we received a refrigerated truck from the Foodbank of Southeastern Virginia. While having these vehicles has expanded our ability to serve our communities, the insurance and personal property tax expenses are still paid out-of-pocket due to a lack of funding.

Back to School

In 2011, I met several parents and grandparents who discussed needing assistance with school supplies and clothing for children returning to school. I started my second outreach program, Back to School Giveaway and Carnival for Grades Prek-12. For the first several years, the event was held at my home on the empty lot on the side of the house. I invited families to receive a backpack, a Ziploc bag with school supplies, clothing, and shoes. Students enjoyed the bounce house as well as a day in the park.

From 2011 to 2019, our Back-to-School Giveaway assisted thousands of students with school supplies and personal hygiene products. Our clothing boutique assisted many children with clothing and shoes. The Dental bus from Washington, DC, gave hundreds of student's dental screenings and dental kits. Recruited a local Doctor in the area; she came out with a team to administer school physicals. The Doctor set up examination rooms using the examination curtains for privacy. The Health Department, as well as Walgreen, administered school immunizations. The Lions Club administered sight and hearing tests.

In addition, students and parents were given lunch. We also had face painting and a bounce house. Beginning in 2017 with the help of the Foodbank, I was able to bring fresh produce and fruits to hand out to the families at Back to School. In 2020 we delivered backpacks full of school supplies to local children that received our daily pandemic meals while being home. In 2021 items were delivered to a local school in the community, a local t-ball tournament, and a partnership with the schools in the community with a day in the park.

Day of Sharing 2011

During Martin Luther King Jr's birthday, I wanted to do something to assist the community as Martin L. King would do. I rented a community center and invited the community to come for a meal and a wonderful time of sharing and learning about the values of the holiday. We gave out new coats and gently used clothing to the community that came out and participated in the event. We had an elected official who came out to the event. It was an eye-opener to her that we had people in need right here in our back door needing essential items such as clothes. I met an elderly lady that never seen a crossword puzzle before; we sat down with her and showed her how to do the word search.

Christmas Warm and Fuzzy

During the Winter of 2012, I noticed children in the neighborhood standing at the bus stop with either no coat or a light jacket. I spoke with my team, and we worked on Warm and Fuzzy. The dream was to assist parents with coats, warm clothing, socks, and winter pajamas. We started small working with ten families. We delivered coats, clothing, and food boxes to last for two weeks while the kids were on Christmas Break. By 2015, we began to have the Outreach at Dr. Clarence Cuffee Community Center, which held over three hundred people in the beginning, and in 2019 we served six hundred people.

We had lines out of the door. We supplied children with brand new coats, clothing, shoes, gloves, scarves, pajamas, socks, underwear, toys, and a warm meal, as well as a Holiday food box. The Foodbank was instrumental in giving away fresh produce and fruits, and the local area hospital would donate Turkeys to give to the community at the event. One year a child cried because she wanted a bicycle but did not win the raffle. One of Buffalow's Family and Friends members purchased one for her and a helmet and delivered it to her home. The child was so happy. In 2020, we held a drive-through sign-up event that served 250 kids clothing, toys, and food items. Warm and fuzzy volunteers include high school and college students, the U.S. Navy, Omega Psi Phi Fraternity, and community leaders.

Mobile Pantry

February 2018 Mobile Pantry began. Every 4th Wednesday of the month, in one of the churches in the community, we utilized their parking lot until 2021. The Mobile Pantry is now located in the parking lot of our pantry. Foodbank truck delivers healthy foods like fresh produce, fruits, and meats to be distributed to the people in the community. We serve 200 families every month with the support of The Foodbank of Southeastern Virginia. The Mobile Pantry is run by Buffalow Family and Friends volunteers.

Buffalow Family and Friends Community Pantry

As stated, our initiatives started in 2010 in my home. All the items we purchased were housed there. There were so many things in our home we could barely walk around; items were even upstairs in the hallway and a dedicated room in the back upstairs. The backyard had deep freezers covered, pallets covered with canned items, and two areas designated outreach items. I received a call in August 2020 that Buffalow Family and Friends would be receiving 4,000 pounds of nonperishable items in October. I went to my mother, and we talked it over; it was time for us to look for commercial space. We located a space available in September, signed the lease, and moved in. The space was extremely limited and full in the first three months. In March 2021, the space beside the community pantry became available. We took another leap of faith and signed the lease for additional space.

The additional space is to be used as a community kitchen where we cook hot, nutritious meals all year round for the senior communities. Having no operating money, just with having faith in the Lord, we opened BFF Community Pantry. The Community Pantry is accessible to the community we serve, going them access to healthy foods. With leasing the space, we are learning the rules to commercial space, how the city and fire inspection goes, changing the use of the building (type of operation you will establish). In this space, we can house our food items instead of using our home, backyard, and personal sheds. Community members come to the pantry to pick up items they need at no cost.

Sometimes I just want to give in and throw in the towel. Then I ask myself, "Who will serve the senior population?" Seniors look forward to our monthly visit; sometimes, we only see all month. They voice their concerns to us, and we sometimes become their advocate to solve their problems. We receive thank cards and post our Facebook group page from seniors saying they love our monthly items.

Many in need talk about what a blessing the pantry is to them. They can come in daily or weekly to pick up several types of food, dish detergent, lotion, and toiletries. My goal is to assist families and seniors with healthy fresh produce and foods. The pantry has assisted with my dream coming true.

Afterthoughts

I look back and observe the many wonderful works that have been done throughout my many years of completing outreach for the community. Senior citizen assistance has been my proudest accomplishment. Just started out delivering them Thanksgiving meals to set up at their clubhouse, celebrating monthly birthdays with hot homemade lunch and birthday bags; now, we delivering them much-needed monthly groceries that include fresh produce and essential items. Sometimes we can do a Popup Clothing boutique for them; they love to shop. Seniors also love to talk, especially when we have youth volunteers.

Starting with one senior community six years ago and now serving five senior citizen communities is a true blessing. Running the nonprofit from home was convenient, and now with a location to operate away from home, it is hard. You must be disciplined, making sure all bills are paid monthly, daily clean up, and monthly maintenance remain priorities. My work and hope to continue for many years to come.

I often have no social time to balance being away from home 8-10 hours a day, sometimes seven days a week. Most times, I turn down going to evening meetings due to the physical labor, and when evening comes, I am drained. Much preparation comes with getting ready to serve each community. Even when I get home, paperwork and follow-up communications often go into the evening to complete.

Future of Buffalow Family and Friends Community Days, Inc.

In years to come, I hope to have a large space to operate from. We envision a space where families can sit and have a meal and wash their clothes. Also, a Senior drop-off service, where we would prepare hot meals and provide crafts and other activities for them during the day while their family member is at work. We would also like to incorporate a few hot meals with their grocery bag and essential items. We hope to expand our delivery to all senior communities weekly instead of monthly.

To help make those plans a reality, within the next five years, our goal is to secure (purchase or be donated) a building that will house a warehouse and distribution center; a full-service cafeteria; and a resource center. The warehouse will enable us to house fresh foods and deliver products weekly into communities. The distribution center will be where volunteers will come in and make the grocery bags, produce bags, and the essential items bag to be delivered to the communities. We also hope to develop partnerships with local restaurants to pick up their edible surplus food and deliver it to communities. We plan to develop a phone app for individuals to place a food order to support that effort.

In the Resource Center, we will invite local agencies to come and share their resources with the community and have showers and washer and dryer areas. Financially, we will need the stability to pay the operating costs for this facility. The operation includes paid full and part-time staff needed to run these centers. Develop a phone app for individuals to place food pickup or delivery orders.

Lessons Learned

Final Thoughts

If you are looking to start a nonprofit organization, it takes commitment, patience, and hard work; however, it's a way to give back and help those in need. Research your vision, establish the mission of your vision, and have a good support system to help you with your vision. Growing and sustaining your nonprofit will take years. Make sure you are at all events that cover the issue of your nonprofit to tell your story. You must have an outcome to your mission; how are you changing the lives of people you are serving. Buffalow Family and Friends grass-roots effort has successfully mobilized volunteers and partner agencies to respond to important needs within our low-income communities. As a small nonprofit, the challenge of working within low-income communities with great need is to generate the financial resources needed to deliver programs. Even with our strong and steady partners, we stretch our resources with the growing number of needy families. Volunteers keep Buffalow Family and Friends in operation. We have 40 volunteers a month working, knocking on doors serving our seniors. This work is hard; it takes hours and days to serve a community.

As a nonprofit founder, I enjoy making a difference in the individual lives we serve. Boots on the ground serving those in need and eliminating hunger one step at a time is my passion and the reason I do what I do.

However, while operating BFF, I have suffered from several illnesses and surgeries that have required hospitalizations and rehabilitation. While I have always wanted to serve, I physically could not participate in the program delivery. I feared this would be the end of BFF, but gratefully, BFF's team of core volunteers and partners carried on the mission while I was down. They get the work completed, and we are proud that no senior community has gone unserved. This validates the need to operate with a servant leadership approach and ensure that MY mission is the SAME mission of the team. Then you need to work hard to ensure that they can fulfill that mission. It always comes down to the relationships: the people on your team, the people you are serving, and the people funding your projects. I firmly believe that servant leadership and determination contribute to your success.

Ronjeanna Harris is a native of the Eastern Shore of Virginia now residing in Virginia Beach, Va. Ronjeanna is a wife, mother of 6, and grandma (JeanMa) of 1. She is a full-time Nurse LPN with over 20 years of experience in Healthcare. Ronjeanna is also a Certified Wellness Coach helping clients, customers, and the community with natural alternatives to implement and add to daily lifestyle regimens.

Ronjeanna launched her business in 2018 called *Just Jeanna's Skin Care LLC*. Ronjeanna's All Natural Skincare Products and Services quickly emerged, serving people locally, nationally, and internationally. Her products are in a local beauty supply store called Lips Beauty Bar & Supply in Norfolk, Virginia, and Walmart marketplace USA/Canada. Ronjeanna's services include skincare and wellness consultations, focus care, and order customization.

Health and wellness education is important to Ronjeanna, and she prides herself on serving and giving back to the community. Ronjeanna's community service has a long history dating back to being a kid alongside her mother on the ESVA. Ronjeanna started her nonprofit Jeanna's iFeed in May of 2020. Ronjeanna currently feeds weekly families and seniors in need of cooked meals. Through Ronjeanna's nonprofit, she serves the homeless community monthly with cooked meals and essentials.

Ronjeanna launched a FB live talk show in September 2020 called Just Jeanna's Skin Care LLC Health Wellness Tips & Talk Show, where topics are discussed, covering four key points from a nurse's point of view!

Ronjeanna Wellness Show transitioned to Amazon fire and Roku TV in April on the BigMind entertainment channel. Ronjeanna is a published author of "I Stumbled to Rise inPurpose!"

Ronjeanna's business and nonprofit are faith-based, standing on the principles of God. Ronjeanna is an active member of Cornerstone City of Refuge Ministries International, aka "The New City VA," under the leadership of Senior Pastor Apostle Dannie Ducksworth and Pastor Elder Rebecca Ducksworth.

Serving *in* purpose is number one in everything Ronjeanna does; In addition to giving back and helping others. Ronjeanna wants to encourage and help others to discover their full potential.

PURPOSE IGNITES SOLUTIONS! A NURSE'S JOURNEY TO THE NONPROFIT WORLD

I would often get overjoyed as a kid when I saw the amazing outcomes of troubled situations people would overcome. I was always different and felt the pain of others, not knowing a clue of my purpose or assignment back then. Later, life's journey made it clear. Helping others in their daily lifestyle journey was a passion I could not shake. As I emerged into adulthood, I would drive through towns and neighborhoods, seeing people in underserving areas struggling with minimum to no solutions. During times of my life, I experienced tough times because of life's uncontrolled issues. I was a single mother incredibly young and did not want to depend on anyone. So, what did I do? Jump headfirst into the world unprepared. I got a rough start but managed to finish high school, go to college, and later become a nurse. So, I was able to identify with individuals' struggles and setbacks that they would encounter. I love helping and encouraging people, but most of all, I love seeing realistic solutions provided.

During the early onset of the pandemic, I witnessed a pre-existing issue that was rapidly growing. Even with all the services offered in my area, the demand still seemed to be intensively great. Individuals and families were facing severe hunger in poverty and low-income communities. I started, in the beginning, researching the target areas needing cooked meals. Keep in mind that services normally offered were starting to shut down due to the pandemic, and food insecurity was already a demanding issue before the pandemic. I collaborated with other businesses to assist families with healthy meal options in communities facing hunger. I kept seeing that families and individuals could not prepare meals for various reasons. Examples like displaced living in a hotel with no stove or health issues made it unsafe to prepare meals for themselves or their families. These individuals were most times the backbone of the family, so if they were down, the household would go without meals. I also discovered how the options that the undeserved did have were not healthy for them. Many of the candidates had health issues like Diabetes and Hypertension. I was a nurse and knew how to cook. I started creating healthy home-cooked meal options to serve the community, and I was able to mass-produce this service.

I discovered I could provide a solution to target several areas for the families I was assisting. This took reign in April 2020 with just a couple of families. I was still working as a nurse now remote and had my business. I would prep and prepare according to the health and number of individuals in the household. The beginning Recipients had complex needs, which I later discovered went beyond just a simple meal. They were survivors still in the struggle. Hope was starting to look realistic to them, and then something would shatter their moment of possible relief. The recipients wanted to see realistic trustworthy assistance to their needs. Many individuals in need were over organizations and businesses going live when service was being rendered; they started going without feeling like they were a showcase. All the time, solutions keep ringing in my head. The nurse in me knows that for every 'problem or concern,' there must be a corresponding solution. This was especially important to me. I know how it felt to be given false hope, and I wanted to decrease the potential chance of a person going through that.

My strategy in serving had to be purposeful and realistic to the recipients being serviced. Looking at the statistics, according to feeding America, 42 million people (1 in 8), including 13 million children (1 in 6), may experience food insecurity in 2021. I am big on research and studies because people's lives depend on our skills, knowledge, and critical thinking decisions with my line of work. I saw how something simple as a meal could impact the dynamics of a person's moment or day. Proper nutrition is a source that must be fulfilled correctly. The body operates and functions according to what is or is not consumed. The thought of communities with increasing hunger insecurities was hurtful. I could not sit around not doing anything, especially being someone who once struggled to put food on the table when I was a single mother. I wanted to educate in wellness along with providing meals. Why? Because they really go hand in hand. Recipients under the program needed to be educated, given hope, strategic positive insight, and that is just what I was equipped to do.

My nonprofit also is directed by faith base biblical principles. So, I embrace guidance from a Godly spiritual aspect. People want to be able to trust and know they can count on your services. I would often talk to seniors and families in poverty-stricken communities to get an insight into their concerns on a day-to-day basis with the progressing situation of hunger insecurities. The majority of the answers were similar. They would say, "People think we are ok, but we are not." This was heartbreaking to hear, but I understood, having dealt with the same issues. Most people knew how to wear their hardships well. This I know because I used to be one of those people. Assuring trust and confidentiality was another important factor. No one was exempt from falling on hard times. Sometimes shame would form, causing full recovery to overcome the struggle not to happen. So, a meal delivery would become an embarrassment to people for fear of helpers making the recipients a showcase. I wanted to calm that concern to the community I served with a solution of confidentiality. This was a great way of relief to people requiring cook meal deliveries in the community.

Jeanna's iFeed purpose is very profound and meaningful, addressing one's effective wellness, promoting life balance, and healthy eating. Decreasing process meal options and creating a variety of fresh, even local ingredients and produce brought a great impact. Individuals in the community face many other issues, including hunger insecurities in their homes. Many times, health conditions increased the demand, which led to employment issues. The boundaries progress from low income to no income for many in the community. Households of 4 to 10 did not have enough to receive EBT benefits. The concern would bring me back to the thinking table. I pondered, what other programs could I create with positive & realistic solutions?

Jeanna's iFeed serves single mothers, low-income families, seniors, displaced individuals, and the homeless community. These recipients are in low-income and poverty-stricken communities.

Food insecurities were always a major issue not being resolved in America, and the pandemic just made it more recognizable. We currently operate out of Virginia, serving three cities in the Hampton Roads area every week: Chesapeake, Virginia Beach, and Norfolk. Now Jeanna's iFeed serves on the Eastern Shore through collaboration and partnerships. We will travel beyond our service area if requested, and we can safely serve solutions. Jeanna's iFeed wants to ensure everyone we serve that safety, trust, and consistency are a priority. We wanted to be a part of changing the trajectory of food insecurities in low-income communities.

Our programs originally started off providing weekly cooked meals to the community. Later, we found through recipient evaluations and follow-up that other concerns needed attention. That information took us to scale and broaden our services and programs tailored to the community. Jeanna's iFeed really started researching to ensure that concerns could effectively be addressed through our programs. Their concerns raised my determination to approach everything concerning the community we serve as if it were me or my family that needed the assistance. Jeanna's iFeed got right to development and was able to add more services along with having available resources to provide if requests went beyond the scope of what our organization provided. Programs include weekly meal delivery, virtual wellness education classes, nutrition health consultations, military development care packages, monthly groceries & essential items services, and displacement resource assistance. These services are done with certifications, expert knowledge, experience, proven effective strategies, and required ongoing training in our organization. Everything was done authentically with originality.

Jeanna's iFeed mission is to serve the community and beyond by providing cooked meals, wellness education, essential needs & resources to families, individuals, and the senior community in need during difficult times.

Giving back is fulfilling on so many levels. Serving is always a joy and knowing I can do this through our organization and impact the community is humbling and exciting. We wanted to give a simple and concise purpose of the mission so that all who researched our organization would understand.

I look forward to assisting, bringing something so needed and helpful to the community. I get the testimonies and am just thankful to God for allowing me to serve His people in the community.

Jeanna's iFeed services are tailored to provide solutions. We are unique and scaled to give consistent results for the duration of the recipient's time in our programs. We aid in helping recipients get back to their baseline of living; Giving the recipient the boost to feel comfortable in their journey to get to the lifestyle their want to achieve one meal and encouragement at a time. Jeanna's iFeed is big on collaboration and partnerships to expand our reach to serve on a greater scale. Our organization can also mass-produce cooked meals for community events and requests for routine services by partnering organizations and businesses.

Most importantly, we serve with integrity and deliver excellence to the community. It is especially important to me, as the President of Jeanna's iFeed, that the 'servant approach' remains the focus. I have been where the recipient that we serve has been, and it's not a happy feeling; frankly, falling on hard times can be exhausting and mentally draining. However, even with dealing with a rough patch in life, don't stop. What I have discovered is that our recipients have detailed, unique needs. Our recipients are people, human beings that must see that their dignity is considered. We set the bar high in the community with our programs because dynamic outcomes with recipients regaining their worth are our goal.

I look at individuals in underserved communities, and their hearts cry out when you look into their eyes. This really ignites the force to create trustworthy solutions for the community. Jeanna's iFeed goals are to expand By opening branches in the DMV MD area and create more educational services to the recipients and communities we serve. I want to be able to serve all the Hampton roads; right now, we serve 3 of 7 cities. My desire is to grow an organic structured organization with an instant assistant for rising concerns brought to our attention—services along with hunger, crisis, housing programs, and job placement. Workforce development is especially important as an employee and business owner. The low-income community needs more education in areas like mindset structure, reemerging tactics for transition, and focus consultation services to keep them from revisiting the same circumstances—collaboration serving in different states as God directs me.

Jeanna's iFeed services and programs have positively impacted our recipients. They gave reviews such as, "You showed up when no one wouldn't!" Some of our recipients were able to get their families back to a healthier lifestyle through our meals and wellness education. Trust was built, so recipients did not quit our program. Recipients got the help they needed and received our council that helped them to recover, heal and resurface back into society effectively. Services help ease mental illness triggers enhanced through stress and worrying; hope was restored.

Benefits of becoming Jeanna's iFeed sponsor or donor include assisting in creating hunger solutions, expanding wellness education, equipment needed to effectively serve in the community, assisting in providing a safe haven for recipients to do the intake process serve in excellence properly. Sponsorship and donations assist with required materials, training, and research needed to enhance and better serve the community.

Evidence of Impact

One of Jeanna's iFeed recipients at the time was currently in our weekly meal delivery program. They were experiencing a hostile situation in the current low-income housing they were living in, which eventually caused the recipient to be displaced because of constant break-ins and move to a more stable area because of financial hardship. The recipient had health conditions that caused disabilities that prevented stable work. This put the recipient in a situation that led to hotel living which became overwhelming. These individuals' finances were decreasing and paying for hotels daily was becoming unrealistic. Then one day, their money did not post, and no grace was not given to this disabled recipient of our program by the hotel management. Jeanna's iFeed received a call that could not be ignored nor put to the side until later. One of our recipients was out on the curb had fallen from losing balance while being in the heat. It was at that time that Jeanna's iFeed team was alerted, and a decision was made to provide a solution to secure the shelter and safety of this recipient. Jeanna's iFeed team gathered the funds via donations to secure immediate shelter for a week with meals and essentials. The recipient could relax, destress, focus on health, and get health concerns addressed. During this process, we provided resources and assisted in steps to start preparing for the transition to permanent housing. We have programs in place, but not limited to addressing needs that may involve the safety of an individual that is one of our programs. This situation being on the streets was not an option for this person. This provided hope and built faith to keep pushing and fight to have a better life. Who is to say what couldn't have happened future-wise with this individual if Jeanna's iFeed did not go the extra mile that day? The recipient stated they were at a point where they just could not take another disappointment. But because of Jeanna's iFeed assistance in deeming an emergency, the recipient was able to regain the willpower in believing there was a reassurance to keep going during a rough and unsure time in their life. Stability was established.

One of the many unique things about Jeanna's iFeed is that the founder took the approach of "if presented with a problem, it's imperative that a solution be provided in excellence." We also gained trust in the individuals we serve by assuring no live recordings or pictures while serving to ensure safety. There is a structured wellness approach with our weekly meal delivery program. We tailor to the recipient's need, which requires customized focus to directly address the recipient's circumstance to successfully come out of struggle and hardship. Jeanna's iFeed can mass-produce cooked meals to the community. This has landed several partnerships and collaborations for us. Being in health-care has taught me time management and prepping on another level, along with growing up in a household where preparation and accountability were heavily taught. Frankly, there was no room to lack when it came to the serving. Every minute counts.

The Visionary of Jeanna's iFeed

I was born and raised on the Eastern Shore of Virginia to Dea-con Ronnie and Minister Barbara Smith. I am the oldest of 4 siblings. No stranger to hard work, I was active even at an incred-ibly young age serving and helping others, working alongside my mother in the community serving the seniors in the nurs-ing home when I was eight years old. Later as the years would pass, at about 13 years old, I started volunteering summers at the local nursing rehab center in the activities dept. Duties included helping seniors with activities, limited ADLs, passing ice water, taking, and assisting residents in day room activities. This was required to teach us the importance of having a servant's heart to assist others during times of need. Becoming a mother at a young age was a huge eye-opener for me. My family made sure I finished high school and graduated. Not wanting to be one of the statistics went to further my education. Later went on to become a CNA/GNA healthcare career started was working in Maryland 3-11 shifts. I was still determined and continued to climb the healthcare ladder, becoming a medical assistant in 2002, then further proceeded to become a nurse and completed the LPN program in 2009. I love teachable moments, which kept me eager to learn and help be a solution in healthcare. I worked in several positions because of being flexible and available to be able to assist in the demand of nursing. With much prayer and direction from God, I launched my business Just Jeanna's Skin Care LLC, in 2018. I had a great experience personally and in her line of work with the struggle of skincare and body care. Solutions provided work temporarily and created other health concerns because of ingredients which led to creating and formulating safe, natural products tailored to the individual in need of service to their skin. I developed a strong nursing background with years of skilled experience, and she went back to school to become a certified wellness coach to serve her growing clientele better. It was important a be strategic in my approach to provide skincare services to clients and customers with the niche' of customized order options.

I am a committed servant, a kingdom evangelist, mother of 6, wife, and grandmother of 1 beautiful granddaughter. I'm currently working as a pre-auth nurse, running a thriving business that hosts products and services. Just Jeanna's Skin Care LLC health and wellness tips and talk show which launch in 2021 on Roku and Amazon TV. I'm currently the president of Jeanna's iFeed organization, which assists the community weekly in high impact. With great honor serves and is an active member of TNCVA under the leadership of the honorable Apostle Dannie Ducksworth and Co-Pastor Elder Rebecca Ducksworth. I must continue to research, attend workshops, seminar and obtain further education to enhance services in the business.

Balance and structure are important factors to be effective in serving, business, household just life altogether. The main thing is a strong solid prayer life. Prayer is the foundation for me. I prep in advance a lot. My days and weeks can be jam-packed, so every detail of the minute counts. I really utilize my planner more than ever now. Regularly reading my bible helps keep me balanced. Also, it helps me to communicate regularly with my family and my Jeanna's iFeed team giving them tasks to take some of the load off. Now still, time will be hectic, but you learn to push through. Effective self-care is important and a must. Learning to understand your body, eat right, refuel, and remember you cannot pour from an empty cup.

Collaboration Creates Positive Impact

I want to share a few nuggets that will help you define how to make an impact effectively.

- **Define your Purpose**
- **Be intentional about the success of your role in collaboration**
- **Develop teammate character**
- **Communication**
- **Growth for higher levels of team effort assignments**
- **Have a diverse mindset**
- **Know that all cultures and communities' values are uniquely different**
- **Make impactful the face of the mission/assignment**

I pray for sound intentional guidance to help me be the best service to the need of the collaboration that God directs me to be a part of. Learning to position to serve in full capacity to assist the community's need most times leads to collaboration. Its pieces to the execution of the assignment or event can only be effectively mastered by unified team collaboration. I always keep resources up to date to best serve recipients in the community. Connecting with like-minded people is important. Now, like-minded perspectives to broad because those people may be from a whole different walk of life, state, or even country. But still can have a posture to collaborate as a great team player for community-serving.

Never put a limit on the success of the unity. I want to let all who read this know that a life-changing impact depends on having a conditioned mind to increase collaborative flow to better serve. Helping others is a passion that will sometimes require you to shift to address the full measure of serving in the community. Be observative when collaborating with others. Learn to access triggers, strengths, and weaknesses to ensure all team collaboration is making successful progress. So, I also want to add that being collaborative with others can help make the world a much better place for the society that we are in during this day in time. Unity in love will make serving the best impact ever during community collapse partnerships and other projects. Giving back becomes greater to build out when we come together. I even notice it impacts the ones serving. We build a deeper enhanced desire to make sure all bases are covered to reach the need in the community. Organizations get received more when the community sees when or can successfully serve in unity. May these nuggets inspire you to refine and define your reach for your purpose to serve in the community even more.

Remaining Unstoppable

I had to position my mind not to let nothing disable the zeal of my 'why.' I know you are wondering, "What does that supposed to mean?" Well, at the beginning of a nonprofit, business, or assignment, many are super excited. For some people, as time passes, frustration and life issues tend to consume and push the excitement to the side. I have had those moments, so understand that they will come. Here are a few things that keep me stable and motivated.

- **I keep God first.**
- **I pray and stay in my word (reading the bible). Everything you need is in the word of God.**
- **Read motivational books.**
- **I remain teachable.**
- **I remind myself that this truly is not about me or my feelings. Jeanna's iFeed is a movement that is bigger than me.**
- **I also consider the community how our services and programs are needed.**
- **I review my journal and the goals and reasons I cannot quit.**
- **Always surround yourself around like-minded people.**

We must remember that our children are watching and do not want them to think that soon as things get hectic, they just stop. No quitting is not an option. Whatever God gives you that is his will, provision is always made. I am a witness to this.

Starting a nonprofit must be well thought out. The best advice is to write the vision as Habakkuk 2:2 in the word. Seek direction from God and do your research. Take classes and get the training to run your nonprofit properly. Look at the requirements and laws of the state you're looking to launch your nonprofit in. Find a good, trustworthy mentor. Study the organizations that have a longstanding history of stable impact. Also, check out the organizations that are pivoting. Gather impactful guidance and insight to help you be a thriving service to the community through your nonprofit organization. Make sure the individuals that join your nonprofit as board members are in alignment with the organization's mission. Be ready to work hard to build and scale to accomplish the purpose of your "why." Again, put God first. That will keep your nonprofit/purpose growing. Remember, nothing is impossible. Have BIG faith. There are absolutely no limits.

Things to remember!

- Make God's will the focus in anything you do.
- Never doubt your place in the world to make an impact!
- Always believe in your 'why' no matter what life throws at you.
- Be intentional in making an impact to serve others.
- Be bold but have a servant's heart.
- Remain teachable.
- Know that your worth has an impact to help others.
- Stand in great character for those you serve.

Tanikwa S. Matthews is a God-fearing mother of four boys affectionately known as her "Fantastic Four." She serves as the secretary, dance ministry leader, and youth minister at Restoration Outreach Healing Ministry. She is also the CEO and founder of HisNHersJewels, LLC. Her specialty is to create custom designs for him and her to stand out. She volunteers with the high school band and is an assistant chaplain with Kappa Epsilon Psi, Military Sorority Inc. HR Southside Chapter. She is a Master Sergeant with duties as a Victim Advocate and Senior Human Resources NCO proudly serving for over 25 years in the U. S. Army Reserve.

Her drive to motivate, mentor and collaborate with women has birthed the organization Women Achieving Victory Everywhere (WAVE). Initially formed in Kuwait while on deployment, WAVE hosts various events and workshops to help encourage, empower, and uplift women from all backgrounds. Through these collaborations, the motto "Bridging the Gap" was used and has become the overarching topic for Wednesday midweek podcasts. She enjoys singing, bowling, traveling, reading, helping others, and spending time with family and friends in her downtime.

WAVE

Teaching, training, and mentorship are my passions; I'm a lifelong learner! I've learned in Colossians 3:23 NIV, Whatever you do, do it enthusiastically as something done for the Lord and not for men, knowing that you will receive the reward of an inheritance from the Lord. You serve the Lord." Another one of my favorite scriptures for motivation is "And let us not be weary in well doing; for in due season, we shall reap if we faint not." Galatians 6:9 KJV

In the Beginning

Drink water, embrace the challenge, suck it up, drive on, and be all you can be just a few of the words that were drilled into my head over a period of time. As a matter of fact, we chuckled when leaders told us if they wanted us to have a family, they would've issued us one. After a while, I realized the importance of having a solid mentor and accountability partner, often referred to as a "battle buddy." You see, good ole Uncle Sam wanted us to look alike, walk alike, and even think alike. Sharing a realistic point of view with leaders seemed to be few, far and in between, or simply nonexistent. And most of the duty assignments I had, women were rarely asked for their opinion/viewpoint about accomplishing tasks.

Searching for Answers

I've always been rejected for one reason or another. My complexion, hair, size, clothing, whatever anyone could think of, honestly. I had complex and huge self-esteem issues. The Army looked at us as "green" or, in other words, all the same. News-flash, we are not the same, not by far. We were a large, diverse pool fused together to accomplish a mission with mindsets from every religious, physical, cultural, and mental background you could imagine. I recall searching for people to connect with minus scrutiny and backstabbing because I had experienced that my entire life. I kept thinking, where are the real people who don't mind telling you the truth? Is the entire Army like this? Are there any women who have achieved success? Throughout my 25 plus years serving with different units and across a large span of the Army, I noticed a small group of women leaders.

Further in my observation, I made mental notes of women juggling work and home. Most of the women in any leadership position were single and raising their family with the village of battle buddies they'd met along their career. As military women, we make many sacrifices, and we miss birthdays, holidays, school functions, and a host of other things. We move around like a hot potato and are forced to readjust quickly to the new environment.

In 2018, I went on my first deployment to Kuwait. No support channel. Just battle buddies, leaders, and a few duffel bags of things I may need while there. Little did I know I was in for a huge surprise. Now I had been away from my family because we lived in different states. But I've never stayed away longer than eight weeks from my fantastic four. From the eight-hour time difference to seeing nothing but sand, rocks, and concrete barriers, let's not discuss the 110 plus degree temperatures. I was miserable! At the time, there were only 22 females in our unit…22! We had to prove to our fellow brothers at arms that we were just as capable of balancing working life as they were. Sadly, it was not as easy for most of us as for them. A few of the young ladies would come and share their stories with me. We would work together to figure out how to overcome situations. After a while, we began to depend on each other more. We started having women's weekly sessions, workshops, positivity pledges, and even mentoring and praying for each other.

Gaining Some Ground

After a few of these sessions, I spoke with our Brigade Command Sergeant Major (CSM) and asked if we could have an all-female color guard. She said, "Make it happen." I was reminded in Proverbs 31:29 NIV, "Many women do noble things, but you surpass them all." Now I had been selected to the prestigious position of Color Sergeant and led three prior color guard details up to this point. It wasn't until the evening before the change of command ceremony when CSM told us we would be the first all-female color guard in the theater. Emotions running wild, we conquered it. Our hearts were filled with victory from making this historical footprint. We regrouped to take things higher and see how many more "firsts" we could achieve.

So, we decided to host an event for Women's Equality Day for the entire post (base). Sadly, we believed we would get some pushback trying to host this event; one of the chaplain assistants helped get the word out and get the idea approved up the chain of command. Our original idea was to host a tea party. Then we started to look on a more realistic scale. Our idea changed from a tea party to a vision board party. Finally, we hosted an event highlighting woman who may have been the first in their area or career field. You know, Phenomenal Women just like us.

We stepped out of our comfort zones and began interviewing women in leadership, balancing life victoriously. The acronym WAVE was given to me in a dream and the description WOMEN ACHIEVING VICTORY EVERYWHERE. I was ecstatic! This defined all of us. Our group made our list of guests, and we gathered nerves to ask our division two-star general to be our guest speaker. She declined but agreed to do an interview. Once she finished the interview and asked how it would be used, she told us that she would be attending VICTORY! Many of you may not know the impact this had on us. But let me tell you, if you can have a two-star general clear their schedule and attend an event hosted by predominately junior enlisted Soldiers, it is a very big deal!

We immediately went into hyper-event planning mode. We couldn't wait to get off work to meet and discuss new ideas and what we would do at this phenomenal event. Now don't get us wrong, we still missed our family. We cried, laughed, cried some more, and some of us had lost loved ones during the process. Coming together and being there for each other in times of crisis was instrumental in helping us through the consistent negative words spoken by leaders and being away from our family support.

Hosting an event of this magnitude brought us closer together. So much so that we had people volunteering to help with the agenda, preparing our programs, passing out flyers, and sharing the event's news with people across the post.

Honestly, we didn't believe very many people would show up for our event. They didn't know us from a can of paint, our purpose, or our plan for the organization. None of us would imagine our "little" event had been announced on the loud-speaker and shared in various formations throughout the post. VIPs and various senior leadership showed in large numbers to support us. Wow. We bridged a gap between officers and enlisted and recognized some phenomenal women. As Alicia Keys song Girl on Fire was sung by one of our very own board members, smiles reached across the seats in the chapel. We had achieved another victory.

WAVE is an organization created primarily for military women. The overarching intent of the organization is to empower women across all branches of service in diverse environments. We will continue to encourage and uplift them, our purpose is to embody the principles that they CAN be victorious in all situations. Philippians 2:3-4 NIV reads, "Do nothing from selfish ambition or conceit. Rather, in humility, value others above yourselves, not looking to your own interests but each of you to the interests of the others." Let each of you look not only to his own interest but also to the interest of others."

Although circumstances and situations arise while away from our main support system (family and friends), WAVE is designed to help bridge the gap towards success in all areas of our lives. Our mission is to reach all military women and spread the organization internationally. The focus is to continue working with other veterans' agencies and women's groups. We want to ensure all women are setting, meeting, and obtaining their goals.

We can achieve victory spiritually, financially, mentally, and collectively.

Empowerment bags/packages will be given to our deployed women. And for women returning home from deployments, we're working to have welcome home packages ready for them. You would not believe that we receive a large number of care packages while deployed, but hardly anything when we come back home. I know a little backwards, right? Well, that's why we want to change the dynamic, and this has become a focal point. Besides hugging my fantastic four, I remember that I needed a serious date with the nearest spa. So, spa gift cards with massage, pedicure, manicure, and facial are a must for our "EmpowerHER bags." Another huge area of concern is reintegration with the family.

The Soldiers returning home after September 11th started having major readjustment issues. Some committed suicide, others didn't know how to connect with family, so divorce became popular. This needs to change. We are connected with counselors to help with family support, finances, and various mental health issues helping to expand our reintegration program. A few of the counselors are prior military with insight and can relate to most growing concerns without bias.

Bridging The Gap

Another part of our reintegration program is to have previously deployed women in working groups with assigned mentors and accountability partners. Basically, a 'battle buddy' check within our reach when needed. My main reason for these groups is to help work through the adjustment back to a sense of normal life and not coming home trying to go back to how things were before we left. I made that mistake, and the boys thought I was angry with them. Honestly, I didn't know how to connect with them anymore. I didn't know their sports team favorites had changed; they no longer liked some of the foods from before and were not afraid to use their voices (in a respectful way, of course). I had to relearn at home what I was taught in the Army: *together, we all win; there is no "I" in team and embrace the challenge.*

When we returned home, we were eager to move forward with some of our events while deployed overseas. Unfortunately, living in several different states made this expectation quite challenging, so we tried another approach. We started to have food, drinks, and light refreshments during the day to know who we were and remember our name. This only lasted for a short period of time. We knew we had to get creative, and we had to get creative very quickly. Some of the members began to lose interest, so we reverted to something we did overseas, just on a different level—The positivity pledge!

This time we did the pledge virtually, and it was another victory. We all noticed that the communities where we lived had a very small population of military people, especially women. Therefore, we shifted from our original vision to help accommodate the needs of the people within our immediate community. We hosted monthly wellness workshops, collaborative programs, and several other events to gain support, additional resources and expand our network. Finding locations to hold events in the area became more and more challenging. We were already facing difficulties with getting our paperwork completed to start the nonprofit, and it seemed as if we kept hitting every brick wall there was to find.

Nevertheless, I kept pushing forward. I refused to give up because I saw a need for greater. I reached out to several organizations to find out if we could get placed on the list to assist with some of these deployed women. I wasn't going to allow anything to prevent me from being able to keep the organization going. Since I came home and had to solely depend on strangers who had become friends to help me go through some of the most challenging parts of life, I realized that this organization was imperative to keep going. God knows I wanted to do so much more in my heart of hearts. What could I do? How could I do it? The only military people I knew were the people in my unit, and we now lived in seven different states. So, after we tried, most important, to host different events while on reserve duty weekend, some of us transferred to different units, and others completely gave up.

My mind was all over the place. The valuable resources that I needed to reach were so far away from me they seemed unattainable. How could I let people see the importance of this organization who were not military or from a military background? If they only knew some of the things that we go through as women in the military, they could see and be willing to help. I was lost in thought, confused, and going through a severe depression. Connections had been broken, and day by day, the anger built up because no one could understand what I was going through, and I couldn't understand why they couldn't see that I was hurting and miserable.

The young ladies who came to me for advice from my unit didn't realize they were giving me fuel to keep going every day. Many sleepless nights, tears of hurt from having to put up a barrier so people would not walk over the top of any of us, was all I could remember. Did these young ladies realize how much of an impact they had on me? I had to start reflecting on what I was doing while I was there that helped me cope with being away from family, especially my boys. The care packages came in from all over, not just family but other organizations that sent everything from puzzles to inspirational messages.

I also had positive words to help me focus on the mission. Ability is what you're capable of doing. Motivation determines what you do. Attitude determines how well you do it. Even with all of this, I had mental breakdowns. I missed hearing my boys laugh and cry. I missed our cooking projects. I missed dropping them off at school and those off-key songs we sang and prayers on the way. I missed seeing them wave bye, blow kisses, tell them I love them and have a great day on purpose as they shut the door. I missed doing homework and science projects. I missed surprise lunch visits and movie time. I spent mornings flipping through old pictures and crying at videos I took of my boys. There was no time for me to wallow in my sadness. And I could not share with everyone (so I thought). I simply cried quietly in the shower.

It wasn't until one of my Soldiers went through some things God allowed me to share with her. I told her there were times I second-guessed myself. I was also reminded that you have to go through trials to get the reward. I prayed, Lord, why me? And swiftly He replied, why not you? God created us all to do His work with diligence. We go through situations to help encourage others to make it over the barriers and walls. We are in a time where communication needs to remain effective, and our presence needs to have a greater impact. The light in us has to illuminate so we can help others shine. It's not about us! There are broken women, children, and families waiting to connect with us. We have to be steadfast and immovable and do our part in life. WAVE was designed to bridge the gap from those traumas we get broken from in our civilian ways, habits, and things built back up. We wouldn't leave a fallen comrade (brothers and sisters), and we utilize the same principles and remain professional. We are greater together.

Service members are expected to adjust and adapt to any type of environment. If people only knew the tears that we held back consistently trying to balance life, work, mental health, physical health, spiritual health, finances, and so much more, their minds would be blown. Seriously, we don't have time to pause and reflect on anything. Often, we have to carry on business as usual because it needs to be done by any means necessary. This is why it's very important to have a strong team of women behind you to support, coach, and encourage you when you are going through some challenging times. Oh, and there will be challenging times. You can encourage someone today and be going through something far worse tomorrow. I've experienced it over and over.

Some of the toughest roads I've had to endure were getting in a leadership position, keeping it, and getting promoted. As a female leader in the army or any branch, you are viewed on a different scale than your male counterparts. You know the glass ceiling that is often ignored or somewhat invisible to others. HELLO—it still exists! But I tell the dream killers to lead, follow, or get out of my way. I'm taking back everything the enemy stole from me, plus interest! Take the path least traveled to avoid unnecessary traffic and distractions.

Pushing Through

WAVE will work with childcare agencies home daycare in other affiliate organizations to help single mothers find suitable childcare for their children. They don't need the stress of having to worry about something happening to their children while they're at work. Single women don't get promoted because they don't have the time, childcare, and strong support system to take care of their children. These Soldiers cannot attend the required training to be eligible for promotion to the next grade series because of these reasons. Having a child shouldn't prevent you from thriving and getting promoted. Communication is critical for us to have the right resources available and meet the needs of these women.

We tried to revamp and restructure WAVE to accommodate the needs within the community. Once we returned home, our lives pushed us into different directions, and we disconnected. I was determined not to allow the hard work to dwindle; there was still a need. Therefore, I held workshops, received clothing, monetary and other donations to help meet the needs in the area. But something was still missing. I still needed to reach the women in the military. I felt stagnant because there were so many roadblocks. Then the pandemic came, and I was emptied of creative ideas. Then I remembered it's better to earn recognition without getting it than to get recognition without earning it! Some people believe women are an accessory and not outfit.

January 2021 changed the course of WAVE. God spoke to me in a dream and said to restart WAVE. I scratched my head, cried, prayed, and looked up and said, how am I supposed to do that? Then COVID hit my three older boys and me. God reminded me of my vision and mission statements in my journal time. Go live and be consistent was what I heard. Now, if you're anything like me, speaking in public has anxiety written all over it! Then I realized I had been going live doing jewelry for almost a year. I got excited and said I could do this. Then I got nervous again, thinking, well, what will I talk about? At least I could hide behind the jewelry somewhat and use that as a focus.

You know I went back to prayer, right? Lord, show me what to do. Then God gave me the topics for the podcast, and I asked Him if I should invite guests. And God began to show me people who are subject matter experts in a field related to the topic. He just kept saying, be consistent, doesn't get discouraged or dismayed, for I am with you. I was still nervous but had a sense of peace.

Wednesday's at 8 pm are now a part of my permanent calendar. I was fine every day of the week but would clam up all day Wednesday. Can anybody else relate? Even when I was upset because the viewers were low, I still had to press through. And the times I wasn't in my "fancy space" for WAVE, I still had to show up from the car, grocery store, whatever. To date, I still get nervous. I've learned it's so much more than me. And let me tell you, hear me and hear me well, I am nervous as all outdoors, but God said I had to be obedient and show up EVERY WEDNESDAY.

Growing Through the Hardships

I want to be known as being a person to help women find their voice and not be afraid to speak about their past because it helped make them who they are today. I just want to help as many people as possible and connect resources to leave a mark on history; I am a one-stop-shop resource guru who pushes us out of our comfort zones while using our voices. We always want to erase pieces of our past because of fear. And what is fear (False Evidence Appearing Real)? It's an illusion. Fear will keep you in the 'shoulda, coulda, woulda' phase of life. But the truth is we HAD to go through that to get to where we are today.

There are women to reach. Women in need of resources. Women who are tired or growing tired of doing business as usual. Women need to have a sense of relief. Women need a hug, encouraging words, and a simple helping hand without judgment and fear of being turned away. Some children need their mom to be okay. They need to know their mom doesn't have to stress and worry about what will happen next. I've been evicted, and let me tell you, and this is a horrible place to be. You look around, and no matter how hard you save, something prevents you from having enough. There were many nights I fasted. Other times there just wasn't enough because my children needed nourishment, and I could survive longer than they. I don't ever want a mother to experience what I had to go through. Or have any child hear their mom's stomach growling and for her to say I'm fine, knowing there just isn't enough for everyone.

I want to help break those barriers and bridge the gap from not enough to more than enough. I want to impact the women and families I help have faith, hope, and love engrained and are willing to share with other women. The weekly podcasts have opened doors for me to connect with women from all walks of life. It's given me a sense of joy knowing how many resources are available, from our young teenager writer with books of overcoming adversity for young children to grief and counseling services. Donations for WAVE would go towards a customized care package for mom (spa treatment, hair appointment, massage, etc.), welcome home yard sign from our local business, four sessions of counseling, and a team of 3-4 women to celebrate their welcome home and be a mentor for at least six months upon their return.

WAVE is uniquely designed because its primary focus is the military women and the entire family. Although our target audience is military women, some of the programs we look to offer very soon are literacy programs, domestic violence survivor awareness workshops, financial literacy classes, mental health classes, housing assistance, childcare assistance, and coordinating with local boutiques for clothing assistance. These programs are essential because these are some of the areas where many women are hindered the most. Another focus is for military women transitioning out of the military to help with resume writing, interview skills, and job application searches. While there are programs designed to help transition you from the military, they only touch the surface. More detail needs to be exhibited to help with the holistic approach to transitioning from military work life to a civilian employer. Another area we would like to touch on is those looking to start their businesses, whether profit or nonprofit. These classes will be embedded in the workshops with experts from all different fields, and packets will be provided with information from startups to actually receive a business license.

Some of the longer-term goals are to have these programs offered in a residential setting and virtually for those unable to meet in person. Our main focus is a holistic approach to ensuring there is no stone unturned, and every need is met to the best of our ability. Another important factor is to network and collaborate with community partners and to grow; it's helpful to work with other agencies.

Currently, I'm the only organization whose primary focus is geared towards military women in my community. The great thing about our organization is that our community partners have goal-oriented programs for empowering women. Our approach is to help women become resilient in search daily for a positive approach versus focusing on the situation they see themselves in and altering your mind to see the goodwill help you eliminate whatever negativity is trying to infiltrate your space. Surrounding yourself with positive people that will multiply and add versus divide and subtract are essential tools to daily living.

As a nonprofit leader, there are many challenges that I face consistently. I've heard how there needs to be a healthy balance between work life business etc. I'm not sure about other nonprofit owners, but the balance seems to be a bit challenging at times. Especially when you see a need and you have the ability and resources to supply, the set times for your organization sometimes go out of the window. Do I have a balanced life? I would have to say my balanced life wouldn't be compared to another nonprofit owner's balance because we're two different people with two different business ideas. We must know how to maintain a healthy lifestyle, including eating right, staying hydrated, and most importantly, having a relationship with God. Prayer is just as important as washing your face, brushing your teeth, and getting dressed in the morning. Without prayer and a relationship with God, you could potentially be operating out of order. The things that need to be done have to follow a certain order. Since God already knows the plans for our lives, we need to communicate with Him and be in the right alignment through discipline. Let me say this; I don't operate without making sure God has given clarity to do so.

Victory-The Impact

Bringing the nonprofit to the people is something we must be willing to do. Many people are afraid to ask for help or believe others want something in exchange for their service or good. One of the things a fellow Soldier shared with me is how WAVE had a lasting imprint on them. (Keep in mind we were overseas and the ability to move freely was extremely limited). We did assessments to help reach her with workshops. One of the workshops was the positivity pledge to help her see things from a different perspective. Please note, she was a person who was angry all the time. Part of the positivity pledge was selecting a person to connect with, encouraging, and praying for them for at least 30 days. Praying for someone else and speaking the pledge helped overcome the anger she was holding on to. Then we had a vision board party designed to lay out some things you expect to have manifested. Habakkuk 2:2-3 KJV says it this way, "And the LORD answered me, and said, Write the vision, and make it plain upon tables, that he may run that readeth it. For the vision is yet for an appointed time, but at the end, it shall speak, and not lie though it tarry, wait for it; because it will surely come, it will not tarry."

Another lady attended the workshops before COVID. She was moved and often asked when we would have the next one; we were doing them every other month. She stated she loves the podcast but said there's nothing like face-to-face communication. And when I didn't believe we were making an impact. She constantly reminded me how the program and speakers were helpful. Say it with me—Victory!

Some of the service areas are mental health counseling, grief counseling, domestic violence, sexual harassment, authors, financial consultants, various entrepreneurs, psalmists, and business owners from various backgrounds, including our youth. Many have been guests on the podcast or viewers watching, and they have been inspired and even connected with some of the panelists/speakers for their services. This was the goal to connect the resources to the people and help us all grow together.

These are the tools that keep me going. When I don't feel like getting on the podcast, hosting events, or getting that "no response" I remember that one can chase a thousand, and two can send ten thousand to flight. I have to Get Up, Dress Up, Show Up, and Never Give Up. People are waiting for the services I'm connected to, the available resources, and the skills, talent, and ability embedded in me. I cannot give up because someone needs to know how to make it through adversity. Someone right now has been trying to figure out how to reconnect with their children/family. Someone right now needs to know there's nothing wrong with their choices to join the military. Someone right now needs to know they are victorious and need to walk as such. Someone right now needs to wipe their tears and speak positivity over their lives. Someone now needs to know there is goodness waiting for them on the other side of the bridge. Someone needs to know the gap from when they are to where they want to be is just a connection away. Someone right now needs to use their voice and speak out.

I compressed even more inside by pressing through adverse trials, losing friends, and dissolved relationships. Oh, but when that confirmation came in that clubhouse room, RE-PEA-TED-LY others need to hear your testimony. I've been using this mouthpiece to share and motivate others since—no more hiding from God and no more holding back because of fear. Speaking out helped me realize I was healing myself and regaining strength plus inner peace! So, you heard it from me; my voice will NOT be muted, and I will use it to spread the news of how I overcame trials, heartaches, and pains that almost killed me LITERALLY! Thank you for those family and friends being awesome vessels and reminding me that my voice was given to me to use and not stay on mute!

Let them talk! No matter what you do, how you do it, you will never please everybody. We will always have cele-brators, and there will be haters. Just call it to balance. While they're talking, keep walking; you have to make moves, and the haters are mad. You are not defeated, haven't been beaten, and are not dead. Tiny seeds know that to grow, it needs fertile ground, covered in darkness, and struggle to reach the light until it breaks the soil. What starts as a seed eventually becomes so much more. The seeds are the WAVE vision, the ground is the mission that needs to be carried out, the darkness is the behind-the-scenes collaborations, network and people helping with the vision, and the light is how God increases based on our obedience to do the work. Faith is the substance of things hoped for. It's the evidence of not yet seen. In other words, whatever you believe God can do, He will do. We walk in faith and not by sight.

We are victorious! Let's collaborate and Bridge the Gap together!

Connect with us:

Facebook https://www.facebook.com/womenachievingvictoryeverywhere

Instagram www.instagram.com/womenachievingvictory

Website: https://www.womenachievingvictory.org

Veronica McMillian, M.A., is a native of Chesapeake, Virginia, where she lives with her husband. She grew up understanding the importance of being an entrepreneur and serving her community. Veronica is a Nonprofit Consultant & Trainer; she is known for her uplifting and inspiring presentations on empowerment and love. She is the Founder/President of The Micro-Non-

profit Network Inc., founded to help small organizations grow and provide impactful and effective programs in their communities. Veronica serves on the board of The World-Wide Women's Group Inc. and The Beacon of Hope Inc.

Veronica has over 25 years of experience in education, training, community outreach, program development, and counseling. Using her knowledge as an educator and trainer, she has helped empower individuals and transform organizations. In 2020, Ms. McMillian was awarded the Community Impact Award from The National Council of 100 Black Women Inc. She also received in 2020 the Chesapeake Icon Award from J. Paris Media Group. In 2019, Veronica was awarded the Community Impact Award from Christian Women Alliance. In 2018, Veronica was awarded the MLK Nonprofit Award from Global Ministries. In 2011, Veronica received the TEC Nonprofit Award from The Career Engineer (TCE). In 2009 she was awarded the WHRO Community Leaders Award in Public Safety. Also, in

2009 she received the Commitment to Children's Award from Continental Societies Inc. In October 2009, Ms. McMillian received the FBI's Community Director's Award for the Boys to Men program she created in 2008.

Ms. McMillian holds a master's degree in Human Service Counseling from Regent University. She is also an Adjunct Instructor for Tidewater Community College in Virginia Beach, VA.

THE SEED

I can remember as a little girl always wanting to lead, direct, produce, or have my "own thing." I didn't know if "the thing" was a business, but I liked the idea of doing things exactly the way I wanted them to be. This was the seed, and at that time, I didn't know the seed was entrepreneurship; I just wanted to see my seed grow. My first business was a backyard fashion show. My family and I designed a makeshift stage and hung sheets to act as a curtain so that our audience couldn't see what was going on behind the sheets. My models marched across the stage in their shorts, tennis shoes, and towels hanging from their heads as if they had long flowing hair. Everyone was so excited because my neighborhood fashion show was a huge hit. I was over the moon, and I wanted more!

My second business was eyebrow arching. I made my own money by arching the eyebrows of all the women and girls in my neighborhood. I was in high demand every week, and I loved the attention my business was getting. However, I had no idea that my passion for helping people would lead me to start a nonprofit from those early days to this present moment.

Be Industrious!

When starting a nonprofit or for-profit business, you must be industrious with a "no quit" attitude. My definition of industrious simply means hardworking and researching your industry. Know that you will make mistakes but keep fighting through the hard times. Even when you feel like giving up, keep pushing. It is imperative that you understand and know that you will put your blood, sweat, and tears into your business. The dictionary's definition for industrious is someone diligent and hardworking. The root word for industrious is 'industry,' which means you must have a clear understanding of the nonprofit industry so that you can be strategic in moving your nonprofit forward.

Along with being industrious, you will also need someone by your side to support you and encourage you to keep pushing when you feel like giving up. By having a support system in place, you will be able to brainstorm, collaborate, share ideas, and have someone help you make sound decisions regarding your nonprofit organization. Your support system can also sound the alarm when you get off track or jump a little ahead of yourself. You have to learn all you can about the nonprofit world, which means knowing your key player, the trends, and the policies that will impact your nonprofit. Use every tool you can to stay on the cutting edge of the nonprofit industry. Thank God for my industrious nature!

Wisdom Tip: Grow slow and give the seed time to be nourished!

Know Thy Self

Have you ever heard the term 'mind your business?' This term can be used in many ways, but I really want you to focus on yourself from me to you. I have learned over the years that you must be really clear about who you are in business. I call this "The Me in Business Philosophy." Simply put, it means you have to examine all of yourself. This includes your emotions, motives and intentions, past trauma, unforgiveness, money matters, and communication skills. I know what you are thinking, "What does all of this have to do with running a nonprofit business?" It has everything to do with running a nonprofit because they will deal with you if you don't deal with these things! Let's take a moment to dig deeper into each of these areas. You will find that each of these areas will resurface somewhere in your business life, and if unchecked, they have the potential to be devasting or to destroy your business. Do I have your attention now?

Emotions- are feelings on the inside designed to move you in a certain direction. If you have unchecked or out-of-control emotions, you want to get this under control as quickly as possible. Trust me on this: when you enter into the nonprofit world or the business world in general, you will face adversity, critics, and individuals who don't like you or your business. You can't get angry, blow up, and fuss or fuss curse people out. It's not a good look on you, especially if you are just getting started with your nonprofit business. Do you get what I'm saying? Work on controlling yourself by dealing with your emotions. It may mean that you have to get counseling to help you through, but it will be so worth it and beneficial for your nonprofit business.

Motives & Intentions- Always approach every business endeavor with clear motives and intentions so that you remain focused regarding the work that you are doing with individuals or the community. Your nonprofit mission must be clear regarding the nonprofit programs and services that your nonprofit will provide. I had to learn this lesson the hard way. This is why I'm sharing with you some life lessons so that you don't make the same mistakes I made when I opened my nonprofit business. There will come a time when you will be approached about the programs and services that you offer. Sometimes the people that are approaching you have motives and intentions that can be harmful to your organization, so always proceed cautiously. Never change your mission to fit someone else's agenda, program, or service; always stay true to your mission. Your mission is the guiding force. Know that the nonprofit world is very territorial, and there are a few players who don't want to play fair, share, or collaborate with other nonprofits.

Past Trauma- Clear the clutter and remove all baggage and mess from the past that can be a weight to you. This simply means examining your life and the people that are in your inner circle because it can be detrimental to your business. Again, I know this sounds like a counseling session, but it is the best advice I can give you. When you understand that your future is in front of you, you will remain focused, but if you keep looking back and dealing with past issues, it's counterproductive. You have heard the term 'bad news travels fast,' so you know what I mean when I say clear the clutter and resolve issues so that you can soar in your nonprofit business.

Unforgiveness- is a weight that brings you down, so get rid of it and release yourself from prison. I've seen people lose out on great partnerships in this business because they are still made from something that happened years ago, or they listened to a lie that someone else told, and they believed it. You have so much work to do to grow your nonprofit business, so don't get sidetracked and held back because of unforgiveness. Learn to forgive and move on because you are going to need every ounce of yourself to get through your first five or more years in the nonprofit world.

Money Matters- Learn as much as you can about money. In the nonprofit world, you will always be asking for money, so there are a few things you need to know. You need to understand the cycle of money, how to manage money from your grants and other donations, and you need to know how to manage the money that comes into your organization properly. Suppose you have struggled with managing your own personal money; it's highly likely that you will struggle to handle your nonprofit money. You have to examine yourself and ask yourself, what is my earliest money memory? By doing this, you can uncover areas from your childhood that you learned by watching others handle money. I grew up in a home where money was hoarded, and I was always told that we didn't have enough. Needless to say, I was thinking for a long time that there was not enough, but I quickly learned that I had to change what I was thinking about money. I learned how to manage money because if you don't learn to manage your money, your money will manage you.

Communication skills- Good communication skills will take you a long way in the nonprofit world and beyond. Learning how to listen effectively and share your story in an impactful way will be a game-changer in your life and business. The best nonprofit leaders in the industry know the importance of good communication and relationship building. These two things go hand in hand, so work on public speaking, writing, understanding body language, and not talking too much. If you can learn these skills along with the art of silence half, the battle is won.

Now that I have given you some keys to examine yourself. If you put these things into practice, you will soar because you are not carrying baggage that will weigh you down.

Wisdom Tip: Trust God to lighten your load as you go through the process.

The Helping Hand

I've always been an advocate for helping others. I believe it's the only way a small nonprofit can sustain itself and continue to do good and be a change agent for the community. I really love helping people and seeing the smiles on the faces of people that you help is priceless. As a matter of fact, your organization's mission should always be about helping your community and individuals through adverse situations and conditions that have the potential to keep them from succeeding. Your organization should help the community by lending a helping hand, so everyone wins. I call this the "winning hand." Always remember when you help others, it comes back to you in ways that you couldn't imagine. There is something magical that happens when you lend a helping hand. Blessings will flow because of your generosity.

I must also warn you that there will be those who will try to take advantage of your generosity, so be careful and diligent about whom you support and always know WHY you are supporting them. Always make sure to research the organizations or individuals, ensuring you aren't making a bad investment. In the nonprofit world, the term. 'Return on Investment (ROI)' simply means the outcomes from the money they are giving to support your organization and what impact it will have on the community. This is important because no funder or organization wants to support a dead or dying cause. The goal is to help by lifting up and not throwing money away because of ill intentions, wrong motives, and people trying to take advantage of your generous heart. Listed below is a helping hands flow chart to help guide you through the process of making a difference in the community.

Wisdom Tip: Always know WHY you are helping.

Let's Talk Business

Most individuals will start a nonprofit business because they want to make a difference in the lives of individuals or in the community. There is no greater reward than seeing someone's life improved as a result of a program or service that your organization provided. Most individuals start a nonprofit or business because they are passionate about a certain cause or want to advocate for change in the world. This is a noble endeavor, but you must understand that passion alone is not enough. You must understand how to manage your nonprofit or business from every perspective. What you don't know can impact your business. You must understand how to recruit good board members, provide training, capacity building, fundraising, financial management, organizational change, community engagement, staff and volunteer management, and what phase your organization is in as it grows. This can be a daunting task, and it is not for the faint at heart. As I stated earlier, it takes a nonprofit about eight to ten years to really get foundationally strong, so hold on for the ride. In the nonprofit world, everything you do must tie back to your organization's mission. The mission is similar to a navigation system; it helps set your organization's direction. When the organization's mission is 'off' or is always changing, it's hard to get individual or corporate support because there is no clear direction as to where the organization is going.

Suppose your organization's mission is to empower women and girls. In that case, this must be clear in everything that you do, from marketing, fundraising, community outreach, and social media communication. If that is the mission, stick to it, don't waiver from it, and start talking about something else. Always know that you are being watched no matter how small or large your organization is. Whenever you are trying to see if your mission has an impact or meets the community's needs, always conduct a SWOT analysis to determine the organization's needs. SWOT stand for Strengths, Weakness, Opportunity, and Threats (SWOT). Here's a breakdown of the meaning:

Strengths: S stands for Strengths. What are the strong attributes of your organization? Do you have a strong board of directors, or do you have a successful program that is supported by the community? It could be that you have wonderful volunteers. All of these are questions that highlight the strengths of your organization.

Weakness: W stands for weakness. These are your organization's weak attributes that need attention to grow and expand your organization. These weak attributes can include inadequate social media presence, no website, weak fundraising strategies, poor volunteer management, or outdated computer systems.

Opportunities: O stands for opportunities. You must find every opportunity to get your organization exposed to the community. You can do this by partnering with other organizations that have a similar mission and purpose. You can host a community-wide event, host an internet radio program, or podcast, and get involved in the social justice movement.

Threats: T stands for threats. By this, I mean you must know who your competition is and what they are doing in the community. Funders usually will not support agencies that have duplicate programs, so pay attention to what's going on in your community.

Funders are looking for innovative and creative programs that they can support. Outdated information and not knowing your community is a threat to your organization.

Once the SWOT analysis is completed, the next step is to determine the community's needs. How does your organization determine the community's needs that you will serve? I would like to suggest that you conduct a Community Needs Assessment. I can't tell you how many organizations I've seen doing the same things in the community. This creates a problem for funders because they don't like to fund organizations doing the same thing. This is called duplication of services. Yes, there is an abundance of needs in all communities, but from a funder's perspective, they are looking for innovation and creativity when addressing the needs in the community, so be strategic in your planning for serving the community. It's imperative that you know your organization's "niche" and its impact on the community. Your Community Needs Assessment should provide the following information:

- General demographic information of the community such as population, race, geographic locations, and unique aspects.
- Give an overview of the underlying problems and trends and provide evidence of the impact on the community.
- Collect statistical data such as poverty rates, teen pregnancy, crimes, unemployment rates, poverty, and homelessness.
- Compare and contrast local data with state and national data.
- Who can you partner with to solve the problem?
- How can technology play a role in addressing the issue?

Wisdom Tip: Always remain open to educating yourself about nonprofit management.

It Takes A Team

I'm sure you have heard the term 'no man is an island, and this is especially true when you are running a nonprofit organization. In the nonprofit world, collaboration is key. We toss this term around a lot, but research has shown that most organizations and individuals don't really know how to collaborate. This means you really have to find your community partners, volunteers, staff, and leaders who believe in your mission and support your efforts to serve the community. Funders want to see your organization partner with other organizations, and they want to see who's on your team. Your team includes board members, community advocates, staff, volunteers, other providers, and the recipients of your program and services.

These team members can provide valuable expertise and experience to help your organization fulfill its mission and impact in the community. When you partner with other non-profit organizations, especially if your partnership is part of a grant, always prepare a Memorandum of Understanding (MOU) in advance. The MOU outlines the agreement between the partners or parties involved in the grant application. This document spells out exactly what each party will do, and it is sealed with a signature from all partners.

Always make sure your team includes individuals that can tell your organization's story, so make sure you have someone that can provide the following:

- Graphic designs
- Social Media content
- Podcasts
- Website designs

Wisdom Tip: You can't do it alone. Always have a team

It's About Time: Time Management

I have one last point I would like to make before we set sail that will hugely impact your nonprofit business. What I have learned over the years is that time management is about 'behavior' and not a process. In my twenty-one years of being in the nonprofit world, this term seems to be the one that is most abused.

What do I mean about a process? Okay, I am glad you asked. A process is a way of doing things. For example, you can say Step 1: Go to bed early. Step 2: Put the kid's clothes out on the bed the night before. Step 3: Stop texting at 9:00 p.m. and go to sleep, so you get the picture of what I'm saying. Now, on the other hand, behavior is a different kind of animal because it requires you to change what you are doing for change to occur. I submit to you that this is the real problem.

Here's another example. Let's say your favorite aunt likes to call you every day ten minutes before you have to leave to go to work. You also know she likes to talk for at least thirty minutes. You are now put in a situation where you have to make a time management decision. Do you talk to her or leave for work? You decide to talk with her because this is your favorite aunt and this is what you always do, and now you will be late for work. I mean this when I say it's about behavior rather than process. In this case, you selected your normal behavior rather than going to work on time, which is the point I'm making. It isn't the process that has failed, but not changing your behavior is creating a time management issue that can be devasting when it comes to business. This is a big problem when working with others in the nonprofit world. This could make or break you in the business world. So, remember time is money, and you must always honor the time of others.

Before we close this chapter, let's spend a little more time talking about honoring the times of others. I'm not sure how we got ourselves in this position of disregarding the precious time of others, but to me, it is totally disrespectful, and it says I don't really matter to you. I don't know a person alive that wants to be disrespected, but that's exactly what happens when we are thirty minutes to an hour late for business meetings, events, and church. Things are made worst when there is no apology or explanation for the tardiness. Some individuals walk right in and pretend no harm has been done, but they want to be brought up to speed regarding what they missed. NEWS FLASH! It is wrong, and we have to stop doing this in business, especially in the nonprofit world, because it can make a big difference in whether you get the grant or contract. You tell me, does it make sense to be on time or not?

Time management is a key factor in making a successful or unsuccessful nonprofit business. When we look at the word 'honor," it means to reverence, respect, and appreciate. These are powerful words; just think of how things could change in your business relationships if we honored our time commitments with one another. It would have an enormous impact on the way we do business. Deals would be sealed, meetings would end on time, and individuals would feel respected and valued because you kept your word and displayed a level of respect toward someone else.

Wisdom Tip: Always have moments of rest, pace yourself, and stop rushing.

Launch Out!

Starting any business is never easy, and you will be faced with fear, doubt, naysayers, and critics. Never let these feelings or individuals stop you from doing what you are called to do. Once you have researched your nonprofit sector, developed a strong mission statement, gathered a supportive board of directors, and developed a strategic plan for moving forward, go ahead and launch out! It will seem scary at first, but once you have set sail to change the lives of individuals or a community through your nonprofit, don't look back. Learn from every mistake you make and find a good mentor or coach to help guide you through the rough waters you will face as you grow your nonprofit. Let me also make sure that you are aware that failure is a part of the process, so don't give up and quit because things didn't work out as you planned.

It is also important to reassess, pivot, learn from others in the business, and keep moving forward. As I mentioned to you earlier, it takes a nonprofit eight to ten years to get its sea legs in, so don't worry, keep sailing, and you will get to the other side if you don't give up when things get hard.

Here are a few other tidbits to help you to move forward as you launch out into the deep. Understand that data drives funding, so always get current data when you are writing grants. Make sure you have the right tools for collecting data and evaluating your program. Here are some tools for collecting data:

- Pre/Post Test
- Attendance Sheets
- Surveys
- Self-reporting journals
- Interviews
- Focus Groups

You should always have procedures in place to evaluate your program's progress and effectiveness. I would suggest that you have benchmarks for every 3 to 6 months and adjust as needed. By doing this, you can stay ahead and continue to impact the community. Also, I want you to know that a good annual report on your organization's progress is a good way to keep the community and funders informed on what is happening within your organization.

Wisdom Tip: Take one day at a time and trust the process.

Words of Encouragement

I wanted to take this moment to congratulate you and encourage you to step out and do something that you have dreamed about for years, and now you are finally doing it. Know that what's for you will come to you. Don't allow your past, people, or current situations to hinder your progress. You were made for this, and now is the time for you to do it! When you speak to leaders in the nonprofit world or the business world, they will tell your that there is never a perfect time to launch out. You just have to DO it!

I have been in the nonprofit world for twenty-one years, and I'm still learning new things every day that I'm in this profession, so remain open and always be a student to learn new and innovative ways to take your business to the next level. You are starting this nonprofit to leave a legacy for the next generation of change-makers. This is the dream coming alive for you and the community that needs the services and programs that your organization provides.

Here's to all the women that came before you and all the women that will come after you. There will be many growing pains along the way but rest assured that everything you need will be provided! Your obedience to God and answering the call to do something that will change the lives of individuals and the community is no small task, but you pushed, and the baby is here.

Also, remember you must balance your work life and home life. If you get the two confused, you will remain in a constant state of frenzy, and when your mind is cluttered, you will block creativity, and nothing will get done. Set your priorities to do business within a set time, and when it is up, put it to the side and start the next day again. God should always be first, then family, and then business. Again, grow slow. You don't have to rush; the vision was given to you. If this is true, then the provision will come in due season at the right time and when you are ready. Remember that failure is a part of the process, so don't beat yourself up when this happens. These are the steppingstones to your next level. See you at the top!

Peace & Blessings,

Veronica McMillian

THE BASIC STEPS FOR STARTING A LEGIT 501C3 NONPROFIT ORGANIZATION

First, sit and ask yourself these questions. If you do not understand something, Goggle is your best friend. What vision for your Nonprofit has God given to you? What will your nonprofit do? Who is the population that your nonprofit will serve? Do you have proof that your nonprofit will fill an unmet need in your community? Are there any other organizations already serving the same need you plan to? If so, what will be different about your nonprofit? What sort of people will join or support your organization?

1. **Choose a name.** Typically, the best nonprofit names are easy to remember, indicative of what they do, and sound appealing. The name you choose should be unique and catchy. Goggle and search the internet to make sure there isn't already a nonprofit with that same name. Once you get a name, trademark it. You can do this locally, and you can get a USA trademark. Go to https://www.uspto.gov/ for your USA trademark.

2. **Create a Mission Statement.** Your mission statement should clarify purpose & determine direction, motivate staff, supporters, board, & volunteers, provide a template for decision making, focus energy & attention, and send out a powerful message to the public. They should be clear, concise, informative, welcome participation.

3. **Create a Vision Statement.** Your vision embodies a dream that goes beyond what you believe is achievable. It reflects the apex of your organization's aspirations. Visioning transports you beyond your current reality. Your vision expands on your organization's core competencies, which include everything you've already established: history, supporters, strengths, unique capabilities, resources, and assets. It should also include what you intend to continue establishing as you work toward your purpose. Your vision paints a picture of how your nonprofit organization will look in the future. Your vision employs language that is inspiring. It generates a vivid image in the minds of your stakeholders, eliciting emotion and excitement. It arouses interest while also posing a challenge. Your vision explains the path your organization must take and motivates everyone to work hard to achieve it.

4. **Draft Bylaws.** Nonprofit bylaws serve as an organization's functioning manual. A nonprofit organization's bylaws (or Bylaws and Articles of Organization) are its primary governance document. They are the primary formal documents of a nonprofit or for-profit organization. When the organization is formed, the board drafts bylaws; bylaws will outline how your nonprofit will be run and will supplement the regulations already set by the state corporation's code. It is critical to collect the necessary state laws and ensure that your nonprofit's bylaws are in order.

5. **Get EIN from irs.gov.** EIN is used to identify the tax accounts of those who have no employees. Nonprofit organizations and charities are required to have their EIN

prior to starting a nonprofit organization and filing for tax exemption.

6. **File articles of incorporation.** The name of the corporation, its purpose, the board of directors, the physical address, the main agent representing the business, and other details about the entity, such as whether it will be for-profit or nonprofit, are all listed in the articles of incorporation. In the larger articles of incorporation, each item of information is assigned to a different article. Your statement of purpose, for example, would be one article.

7. **Apply for your IRS tax exemption.** You will file a 1023 long form or a 1023EZ short form. The long form is basically used if you think you will be receiving over $50,000 in donations, and the short form is for organizations that don't plan on getting over $50,000 in donations. You can file them here https://www.pay.gov/public/home.

8. **Apply for a state tax exemption for your state.** Unfortunately, even if you are designed as a 501c3 organization with the IRS, you still must file this form with your state. This is the link for VA https://www.tax.virginia.gov/sales-tax-exemptions

9. **Build your board and hold a meeting of the board.** Board members are the fiduciaries who steer the organization towards a sustainable future by adopting sound, ethical, and legal governance, and financial management policies, as well as by making sure the nonprofit has adequate resources to advance its mission.

10. **Look for grants.** eCivis Grants Network: This is a subscription-based service with profiles for public and private

sector funders. The Foundation Center: This subscription-based service for private-sector funders offers several newsletters, including Philanthropy News Digest. Grants.gov: Here, you can find government agency funding announcements for free.

11. **Fundraise.** Individual giving makes up nearly three-fourths of all charitable contributions. Be creative and think of ways you can fundraise for your organization. I started a tee-shirt line to help bring in funding for my organization, and my tee-shirts help save lives.

12. **Get Sponsors.** Define your target audience for sponsorships. Begin by establishing your target audience for event attendees if you haven't already. Thinking about this can help you understand what types of businesses would want to reach out to the people who would be attending your event. After you've laid out your sponsor levels, compile a list of organizations that serve your target demographic to contact regarding sponsorships.

So, do you think you want to start a nonprofit? Need help? Schedule your free consultation by going to https://leadtransforminspire.as.me/